Schools Council
Research Studies

Parents and
Teachers

The report of the Schools Council project, 'Parents and Teachers: A Pilot Study', based at the School of Education and Department of Extra-Mural Studies, University of Southampton 1972–3, under the direction of Robin Pedley and Paul Fordham

Schools Council
Research Studies

Parents and Teachers

James Lynch and
John Pimlott

Macmillan Education

First published 1976

SBN 333 18972 8

Published by
MACMILLAN EDUCATION LTD
London and Basingstoke

Associated companies and representatives
throughout the world

Printed in Great Britain by
Hazell Watson & Viney Ltd
Aylesbury, Bucks

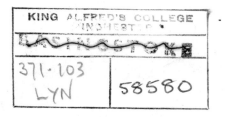

Foreword

The significance of the part played by parents in the education of their children is unquestioned. There has been a tendency in recent years to emphasize the parental role in the early, pre-school years, but although no one would doubt the validity and wisdom of this emphasis, the fact remains that the continued interest, encouragement and involvement of parents throughout the whole span of their children's education is also of the utmost importance. Parents have co-operated with teachers in many ways, ranging from informal contacts, through various types of formal association, to the development in some areas of community schools. However, there are wide variations of opinion on the nature of the ideal parent–teacher relationship and the most appropriate parental involvement in the life and work of the school.

It was against this background that the Schools Council decided in 1972 to sponsor a small-scale pilot study of parents and teachers. This study was of necessity limited to one area, giving it the advantage of depth but also the possible disadvantage of limited generalizability. None the less there are common issues and problems, and it can reasonably be claimed that the area in which the work was undertaken provided the researchers with many situations which will be familiar to parents and teachers everywhere. The object of the project was not to provide definitive answers, but rather, through a restricted but concentrated study, to look closely at the sorts of co-operation and improvement which might be attempted and to analyse carefully the many factors which influence the outcomes. Action-research of this kind presents many difficulties of methodology and procedure, and it is anticipated that this report will make a contribution to knowledge and provide a basis for subsequent investigations. In making it available the Schools Council hopes to stimulate continued informed discussion of a subject which is of great concern to all.

Contents

Appendices

List of tables

Acknowledgements

We have been fortunate in the advice and assistance which we have received from a large number of sources. Clearly such a project as this could not have started without the willing assistance and co-operation of the local education authority and headteachers of the schools concerned. In addition a large number of parents and teachers gave willingly and generously of their time. To all of these we would like to express our heartfelt thanks. Acknowledgement should also be made of the support and comment given over a period of some two years by Paul Fordham and Robin Pedley, and of the effort and imaginative contribution made by our two parent discussion-group leaders, Jenny Arnold and Ada Dickins, who wrote Chapter 8. We should also like to thank Clare Durrani for assembling the bibliographical section and Barbara Smith for assistance with the statistical presentation.

If the result of this report is to encourage an improvement, however small, in the relations between parents and teachers, it will be due to the voluntary effort and enthusiasm extended to the project organizers by the many people who so obviously believed in the aims of the research. To all of these our thanks are offered. Responsibility for any inadequacies in the report rests with us.

James Lynch (School of Education)
John Pimlott (Department of Extra-Mural Studies)
University of Southampton

Introduction

If you ask parents and teachers whether they think that relations between home and school are important and should be improved, almost all would agree. But how can that agreement be translated into action which will improve the service that both parties can give to children in schools? That is the problem with which this report is concerned, for while it would be foolish to assert that the last decade has not seen a vast improvement in the understanding which teachers have of the parental view of education and vice versa, it would be equally naïve to assume that the basis of attitudes has changed fundamentally and to a point where no further improvement can be achieved.

The Schools Council pilot study which provides the basis for this report was undertaken during 1972–3. Its aim was clear and simple, namely to seek to improve home–school relations in three secondary schools. The project was conducted jointly by the School of Education and the Department of Extra-Mural Studies at the University of Southampton.

A pilot study undertaken with a minimum of resources cannot provide definitive recommendations. It can never hope to do more than produce as accurate as possible an account of its activities and results and to present these in such a way as to produce a stimulus to thought, discussion and action in others. It can in addition provide a valuable guide to what appear to be some of the more promising avenues of research which others may pursue and which a major project could follow up. That is the purpose of this report.

There is at the moment considerable political interest in the 'rights of parents', an interest which is capable of exploitation by all kinds of groups for their own purposes. The tempo and stridency of such demands have increased considerably during the last few years, and it would thus seem important to make clear from the beginning that the impetus for our work came from the previous experience both of teacher education and of adult educators working in schools, and a conviction that a major advance in the education of children could be made if more attention and resources were concentrated on the improvement of home–school relations. That such an improvement would involve a rewriting and redefinition of the rights and responsibilities of parents and teachers is apparent. Equally apparent, however, is the truism that rights involve obligations and vice versa. A new educational contract between parents and teachers would need to avoid the hollow assumption that either party can dictate terms. The work carried out in Southampton sought to bring parents and teachers into closer contact and through this to improve the basis of understanding which could facilitate a new partnership between parents and teachers.

How closer contact and understanding between parents and teachers might be achieved is, therefore, the central concern of this report, and the action-research programme which it describes. The well-substantiated view, that the home is at least as important as the school in the education of children, served as our guideline for the development of methods and techniques which would facilitate greater understanding and co-operation. In a sense this is the logical progression, into the parallel curriculum of the home, of the recent rapid advances in the curriculum of the school. The child has to come to terms with both curricula: why should the school not have to do so?

One of our particular concerns was those parents who have the most difficult adjustments to make. The point is frequently made that the culture and values of the school provide fewer difficulties of adjustment for middle-class parents and children than for working-class parents and children. Clearly this assumes a social-class relationship between families and schools which is substantially determined by the economic order of society; and thus the argument is heard that only a substantial change in that economic order can lead to fundamental social and cultural change. Whatever the validity of this argument, it was our conviction that we were not in a position to evaluate this validity when carried to its Marxist conclusion. We would, however, state quite categorically that it is our belief that it is possible to improve home–school relations by adopting a variety of new methods and techniques to bring the educational aims of the school and the social values of working-class families into closer harmony. Such a view rejects the pessimistic argument that only the fundamental political and economic transformation of society can alleviate the social conflicts which exist between home and school, and which militate against educational achievement. It must also, however, reject the cosy if patronizing view that it is the working classes who must do all the changing. A pluralist society has to pay a high price for compassion and tolerance, yet it can only remain pluralist so long as it is willing to pay that price. The pursuit of a monolithic 'uniculture' is not something which British schools have ever sought, nor is it an aim which British society would sanction, even given that it might be capable of achievement.

Adoption of a basic social standpoint that eschewed an ultimate solution made us focus our attention upon parents living in poorer areas, who form the bulk of those parents who rarely, if ever, visit the secondary school which their children attend. But at a time when there has never before been such a heightened interest in education amongst all sections of the community, our concern could not be exclusively with these groups. A higher level of education in society as a whole clearly demands that teachers, when dealing with parents, should have improved skills of explaining and reacting to questioning across the whole social-class spectrum. Thus the schools contained in our work included parents from all social groups usually represented within the state system of education.

Chapters 1 and 2 seek to set our work in the context of more recent developments which have led to the now commonly accepted view of the importance of the home for the education of children. The educational and wider social aims of the project are given in some detail in order to facilitate criticism of the philosophical basis on which the work rested. Chapters 3, 4 and 5 describe the establishment of the project including details of how and why the schools were selected, and a description of the process of consultation which was carried out with all concerned before the project began. Chapters 6 to 9 describe the setting up of the parent and teacher discussion groups, the difficulties encountered and the way in which the groups operated. An indication is given in Chapters 10 and 11 of some of the views expressed by parents and teachers. Chapter 12 then sets out to draw tentative guidelines for future work.

In the appendices will be found a discussion of the concept of action-research (Appendix I), the questionnaires and schedules used in our research (Appendices III–V), suggestions for further reading about parents, teachers and the community school (Appendix VI), and details of some useful films and where to obtain them (Appendix VII).

1 Aims of the project

That clearly defined aims are crucial in any educational enterprise is a maxim that has gained great momentum in the last few years. Not surprisingly, if you do not know what you are aiming for, you seldom achieve it. Yet, from the start, the Parents and Teachers Project was faced with two difficulties which stood in the way of well-formulated and definitive aims. Firstly, there is no neatly formulated recipe for improving human relations which could act as a panacea; and, secondly, people tend to have more commitment to an enterprise which they have been a party to defining and organizing themselves. Thus, from the outset, any set of aims which we devised for the project had to be sufficiently firm to take account of the present state of knowledge in this area, and to enable this to be used as a springboard for action—and at the same time needed to allow for the paucity of that knowledge and the need for a democratic participation of various groups in influencing the development of the project.

In an attempt to overcome this problem, a discussion document outlining our aims was circulated prior to the start of the project proper, which attempted to make clear that the aims would be subject to negotiation between the various groups involved. Our hope was that, if agreement about the work of the project were to emerge, it would be a negotiated arrangement rather than an imposed one.

The initial 'discussion document' *Paper I: The Aims of the Project*, explained that the Parents and Teachers Project was supported by the Schools Council and that two university departments would attempt to focus resources and research on the needs of a number of secondary schools. It described the main components of the project as the parents' group meetings, the teachers' group meetings and the collection and analysis of research data. The sub-aims of each of these components were also given. We consider it important to describe these here in order to facilitate a critique of our work which may help to stimulate discussion and improvement.

The general aim of the project was to study and improve parent–teacher relationships in a number of environmental settings in order to improve the education of children. The argument was that, although we were not working

directly with pupils, an improvement in parent–teacher relationships
was at least as important, in ameliorating the education of the individual
child, as changes in the curriculum, or reducing pupil–teacher ratios, or
raising the school-leaving age. We believed that the attitude of parents
to schools and what they are trying to achieve is at least as important as the
social status of parents in influencing how children respond at school.
While the social context is given and only subject to slow marginal
change, the *attitudes* of parents can be influenced through discussion and
education.

In response to this general aim, we developed four major objectives.
Firstly, we would seek to foster a critical awareness in teachers and parents of
the importance of the home environment in successful child education, and to
increase their sensitivity to the interdependence of the school, the home and
the social services. Under these latter services we understood not just the local
authority social services department as such, but also such supporting agencies as the education welfare officers, legal services and voluntary agencies like
the local community relations council.

Secondly, we would attempt to clarify for parents the values and objectives
of formal education and to encourage them to develop an active interest in
how, what and why their children were taught, and in the importance of the
home environment. We assumed that, although schools themselves have to
change, parents need to understand schools *as they are* in order to participate
in their working and change. There was thus to be some intrinsic 'pay-off' for
parents in learning about present-day schools and how different in many
cases these are from the ones they had attended. In the event this process of
'up-dating' for parents the meaning of school proved of paramount importance, in addition to the other indirect effects the project was to have on
schools.

Thirdly, the project would seek to foster a wider community interest in
educational values and objectives and to assist the school to play an active and
vigorous role in the life and development of the community. Various strategies were adopted in pursuit of this third objective, such as door-to-door
approaches to parents to discover if they would be willing to participate in
discussion groups, and the involvement of local community associations in the
work as it developed.

Fourthly, the project sought to provide teachers and parents with information, intruction and guidance, which would grow into a spirit of self-help, in
order that heightened parent–teacher involvement and a more community-
centred role for the school should be able to continue after the research team
had withdrawn.

In addition to these overall aims and major objectives there were also a
number of subsidiary objectives. The teacher groups, for example, were to
attempt to come to terms with an increased awareness of the social dimensions

of learning and of the teacher's role, and to explore and probe relationships between the social services and the education service which would be of particular use to teachers involved in the differing systems of pastoral care in the three project schools. These groups would work to develop and increase an understanding of the role of the home in the child's learning and to encourage parent–teacher understanding and communication. In addition, they would try to make explicit the different value systems of a pluralist society and to foster an interest in community involvement in education. Initially it was also planned that they would attempt to show teachers the usefulness of action-research into their own school and its social context.

Overall objectives were also proposed for the parent groups, which were to initiate discussion with parents (a) about the formal aims and values of education, (b) about how the schools in Southampton were organized, and (c) about the content and process of development of the school curriculum. The groups would further expect to develop an appreciation of the educational importance of the home and parental influences, and of whether close parental co-operation with teachers and schools could help improve the life-chances of their children. They were to make a special effort to involve social groups which were educationally and socially disadvantaged and to develop an understanding of the role of the social services in supporting and assisting the work of the teacher and the school. Finally, they were to seek to discuss the many ways in which parents could assist the education of their child at home and school, and to consider various means by which parents could be involved in the work of the school.

Work with the teacher and parent groups was supplemented by the collection and analysis of research data. This was designed to obtain information about the present level of home–school relationships in the three schools involved in the project, and in particular the attitudes of parents and teachers. In addition, questionnaires were circulated to both parents and teachers in the three secondary schools. It was intended that the results of the parents' questionnaire would be channelled back to the staff of the schools, on a confidential basis, as quickly as possible. Finally, on the basis of a comparison of the attitudes of parents and teachers to the present initiatives which were being taken in the field of home–school relationships, it was hoped to facilitate future policy-making on the part of the schools.

In the long run, data from the parents'and teachers' questionnaires (see Appendices II and IV) were supplemented by information based on structured interviews with a sample of parents and with the headteachers of the schools concerned (for the parent interview schedule, see Appendix III). In addition, a study was undertaken with all those who participated in the teacher groups, in order to test the effectiveness of the in-service programme: the questionnaire for this inquiry is reproduced in Appendix V.

These, then, were our tentative aims, objectives and proposed methods of work. How these were translated into action we describe in Chapters 6 to 9. In our next chapter we look briefly at some of the arguments for better home–school relations.

2 The importance of home–school relations

The present level of interest in home–school relations both here and in Western Europe has been seen in the context of a number of ideas about social and educational development which have come to us from the United States. Firstly, there was the marked tendency during the 1960s for people in this country to form pressure groups to seek solutions to particular problems. The Consumers Association with its publication *Which?* is a good example of this trend, paralleled at local and national levels in the educational field by the establishment of the Cambridge Association for the Advancement of State Education—later the Advisory Centre for Education (ACE)—in 1961 and the national Confederation for the Advancement of State Education (CASE) in 1962. Attempts were made to lessen the confusion of a plethora of organizations with ill-coordinated aims by the establishment of a Home and School Council in which ACE, the Confederation for the Advancement of State Education and the National Confederation of Parent–Teacher Associations had membership. The decade ended with the establishment in 1970 of the National Association of Governors and Managers.

Secondly, and linked with the first development, was the growing provision of advice and information about education through such organizations as ACE, established in 1963, and more informally through the mass media of television, press and radio.

Thirdly, there was the changing meaning of the word 'school' as understood by the majority of the adult population. In the nineteenth century it had been an institution which had evinced a concern for problems of providing skills; in the early twentieth century it was concerned, in addition, with problems of physical health and welfare; while in the last few years it has come increasingly to be concerned with problems of social health.

Fourthly, there was the increasing impact of developments in psychology and human biology which broadened our understanding of the importance of the early years of life. The Pre-School Playgroups Association began in 1961 and from the start emphasized the importance of the involvement of parents in the educational development of their children. Books for children, and the

Campaign for Nursery Education, also took their impetus from these newer understandings of the importance of early psychological relationships.

Not without a certain justification, the organizations referred to have been seen as predominantly middle class, and arising in the main from heightened levels of aspiration amongst middle-class parents and ideological differences within the English middle class with regard to how these aspirations might be fulfilled. Such developments were also symptomatic of a growing desire for participation which was only in the mid-1960s broadened socially by the impact of ideas on social and educational deprivation which were beginning to spread from the United States, and which led eventually to a redefinition of what equality in education might mean. The focus shifted sharply away from a socially palatable emphasis upon equality of achievement. The idea of positive discrimination, given currency in this country in particular by the Plowden Report,* was one of the most immediate results of this redefinition.

But the underlying hypothesis of the deprivation lobby, though intellectually accepted, could not be popular with powerful middle-class groups who had always seen education as a means of extending their own privilege *vis-à-vis* formerly dominant social groups. Such programmes as 'Headstart' in America and the Educational Priority Area Projects in this country were seen as disappointing in their results although no doubt a useful salve to middle-class consciences.

Soon a counter-attack emerged in the form of polemic in the so-called Black Papers,† the re-assessment of academic study by Jencks‡ and others, and the ideologically highly unpopular arguments of Jensen§ about the innate backwardness of certain racial groups. The idea that academic under-achievement was the result of social and economic deprivation and discrimination was challenged in the renewed debate concerning the proportion of variability in IQ which is attributable to environmental and hereditable factors.

The great debate continues and, whilst it does, those who work in education are still faced with the problem of improving educational provision on the basis of the best available evidence. What evidence there is suggests that, to some extent or another, educational achievement is susceptible to influence through a changing cutural and social environment. We know that children

* *Children and their Primary Schools*: a report of the Central Advisory Council for Education (England), (HMSO, 1967).
† C. B. Cox and A. E. Dyson (eds), *Black Papers on Education* (Davis-Poynter, 1971). The first Black Paper appeared in 1969.
‡ C. Jencks, *Inequality: a Reassessment of the Effects of Family and Schooling in America* (New York: Basic Books, 1972).
§ A. R. Jensen, *Educability and Group Differences* (Methuen, 1973); *Educational Differences* (Methuen, 1973); *Genetics and Education* (Methuen, 1972); 'How much can we boost IQ and scholastic achievement?', *Harvard Educational Review*, vol. 39, no. 1, winter 1969, pp. 1–123. See also H. J. Eysenck, *Race, Intelligence and Education* (Temple Smith in association with *New Society*, 1971).

from higher socio-economic groups tend to do better than those from lower socio-economic groups and that such differences tend to increase throughout primary and secondary education, not least because of different patterns of speech.

The influence of background factors such as living conditions and parental attitudes is crucial to the development of children and their ability to profit from learning situations organized in the school. But just as cultural discrepancies differentiate socially, so do social differences produce differential learning. The power of this cycle in human life remains as yet unchecked, although acknowledgement of the social and cultural impact of impoverished background conditions is widespread amongst both lay and professional groups. Teachers may or may not wish to mitigate some of these adverse preconditions to learning but in the long term any satisfactory results depend on parental understanding, co-operation and involvement. Recent research into the performance of children in selective and comprehensive schools* strongly indicates the way in which educational success under the comprehensive system depends on the support the child receives from home, school and peer group. In the process of the intellectual development of the child the social development of the home thus takes on a *central* and not merely a peripheral role. For if, as has been suggested, working-class authority patterns in the family are a reflection of the non-decision-making, order-obeying roles which they are allocated in society and this is then transmitted to the children of these social groups, the importance to working-class families of involvement in decision-making in education can be seen as a practical way of democratizing our allegedly 'open' society. Viewed in this way, parental involvement in the school can be seen as a useful step in the learning by the child of a pattern of authority within the home which is not a mere reflection of his parents' socio-economic position in society. Similar arguments could be deployed with regard to the child's learning of language, emotional stability and social maturity. In addition it could also be argued that improved parents–teacher relations have a major importance from a social control point of view in providing a child with self-discipline through a dialogue between parents and teachers.

Thus it is apparent that we had 'at our elbow' as we developed the work of the project a wide range of previous work and thought, and a number of basic assumptions which helped to fashion the work which we did with parents and teachers. We assumed for example:

that schools have important social and intellectual functions;
that human thought and behaviour can be deliberately and systematically changed;
that such changes can be facilitated by social research, education and action;

* G. R. Neave, *How they fared: the impact of the comprehensive school on the university* (Routledge, 1975).

that teachers and parents have mutually supportive roles in the education of children;

that these mutually supportive roles can be fostered by the democratic process of consultation; and, finally,

that a small-scale project could do no more than help to stimulate the debate and act as the precursor to a more thorough and extensive series of investigations.

It is on the basis of these beliefs that this report should be understood.

3 Where the research took place

The project took place in the city of Southampton, a city which has a population of 215,000 and is situated at the head of one of the finest natural harbours in western Europe. It has an international reputation as a major passenger and container port. Chalk downland and natural forest areas surround the city giving it a clear physical identity denied to cities which are merely part of a larger conurbation. Over the last thirty years general prosperity has attracted people and industry to the city and to the smaller towns and dormitory areas to the north and east. As in the rest of south and south-east England, population has grown at a faster rate than the national average. Low unemployment, attractive job opportunities, reasonable housing conditions and a pleasant geographical location have attracted people from other parts of the country. An ambitious development plan for south Hampshire envisages a rapid increase in population and a planned development of jobs, industry, leisure, transport and housing. By almost any social and economic indicator Southampton enjoys material benefits which are marginally above the national average.

Most research into education and schools during the last two decades has been concerned, quite rightly, with the poorer regions of the country. It may be considered one of the assets of this particular research project that it was conducted in one of the more prosperous regions, a fact which should make the findings a useful point of reference and comparison when evaluating studies based on disadvantaged communities such as those in Educational Priority Areas. This should not, however, lead us to ignore the considerable variations in income, life-styles and parental expectations for children which are to be found within the city.

The employment pattern of the city is very diverse, as no single industry dominates the labour market. Modernization of the docks and passenger port have made the port a surprisingly small direct employer, its greatest impact on employment being of an indirect nature related to the commercial and ancillary services involved with sea transport. Other main areas of employment are map-making, commercial vehicles, electric cables, automobile and electronic components, heating appliances, hovercraft, ship repairing and the building of small leisure boats. A substantial proportion of jobs is held by people who travel daily from the residential areas of the rural hinterland.

Due to the considerable bomb damage inflicted during the last war, the shopping and commercial centre is modern, spacious and well planned, with much parkland and open space. As in many other British cities, most of what is left of the old housing area of the inner city is populated by coloured immigrants who have stamped their cultural identity upon the terraced houses, shops, cafés, pubs and places of entertainment. Out of a total housing stock of approximately 70 000 dwellings, some 23 000 are owned and rented by the city council. Most of these dwellings have been erected during the last twenty years, in the familiar style of large estates, to the west and east of the city. These estates house people from the now almost razed slums of the city centre as well as people who have moved into the area.

Until the implementation of the Local Government Act (1972) in April 1974, the education committee of the city council had a statutory responsibility for educational standards and policy. In educational expenditure per head of population it enjoyed a national reputation as a generous authority. Levels of expenditure on books for schools published by the Educational Publishers Council in 1972 show that the city was a high spender in this important field. The Council classified the city as a 'good' authority in terms of capitation allowance and book expenditure at primary school level, and at secondary level the city in 1972 was the second highest spender on books out of the 162 education authorities covered by the survey. The pupil–teacher ratio at primary level was comparable to the national average, while at secondary level it was appreciably better, having in 1971–2 14·9 pupils per teacher compared with 17·9 for England and Wales as a whole.

When Southampton Local Education Authority introduced first and middle schools in 1970, it was the first authority in the country to implement throughout its area the recommendations of the Plowden Report on the structure of primary education. Secondary colleges were established in 1967 and were the first such colleges in the country to operate on an open-access basis.

Education in Southampton is now based on first schools (ages 5–8), middle schools (ages 8–12), secondary comprehensive schools (ages 12–16) and open-access secondary colleges (age 16+). In 1973, the city had 25 000 children in first, middle and primary schools, and employed 1020 teachers; 12 500 children in secondary comprehensive schools with 890 teachers; and 363 children in special schools. Only one grammar school (voluntary-aided) remained inside the maintained sector and in 1973 this provided places for 690 boys. Under the Urban Aid Programme, 152 full-time equivalent places for nursery education were provided. The local authority also provided limited financial support to voluntary playgroups and adventure playgrounds.

Clearly the research area is one of relative prosperity with a vigorous, adequately financed and modern educational provision. The deprivations and overwhelming sense of hopelessness and helplessness which educational researchers discover when working in the decaying urban centres of our large industrial cities were not encountered by this project. That is not, however, to say that pockets of poverty were not revealed, but that schools with problems of large-scale social deprivation and racial disharmony are rare in the areas where this research took place.

Relatively prosperous areas similar to Southampton are quite common in many parts of the country, and in many respects they have similar features of large-scale housing developments inhabited by a comparatively young and rootless population; a social culture which is home and nuclear-family based, where the acquisition of material family possessions takes precedence over community activity; and a diversity of available employment which prevents the male solidarity of common employment in a basic heavy industry from emerging.

In short, the research city, in common with many similar places in Britain, possesses a cultural pattern which, despite a veneer of material prosperity, lacks the social cohesion which could, theoretically, be the vehicle for encouraging parents to form closer links with teachers and schools. It is for this reason that one cannot escape a sharp impression in our work that the community school, which is the logical, if not the necessary, conclusion of closer home–school relations, might be achieved more easily in the traditional working-class districts of the older industrial cities, despite their lower levels of educational expenditure and achievement, than in areas similar to those where this project was conducted.

4 The process of consultation

Research into parent–teacher relations is a sensitive area, and in as many as possible of this project great care was taken to consult the individuals and organizations which might be involved. Although ultimately full agreement was achieved, the process of consultation was at times difficult, and some of these difficulties are discussed here, not in any spirit of criticism, but with the aim of setting our research within its local context, and of indicating some of the problems which future projects of a similar nature might find themselves called upon to solve.

It was evident that at all stages close working relations with the local education authority were essential. For this reason the first steps in establishing the project were taken by making direct contact with the LEA at chief-officer level. Initial contact with the chief education officer was made by letter and later by personal contact with the assistant education officer to whom responsibility for liaising with the project had been delegated by the chief officer. The assistant education officer subsequently made contact with schools which might be willing to work with the project, attempting to include a school on a new housing estate (School 1); an inner-city school with immigrants (School 2); and a school with a large proportion of children from middle-class families (School 3). A description of the three schools whose headteachers agreed to participate in the project is given in the next section.

The first initiative towards the headteachers was thus taken by an officer of the authority and not by the staff of the project. (This procedure was later criticized, as some teachers felt a direct approach to the schools would have been more appropriate; we felt, however, that it was important first to ensure that the project was acceptable to the local education authority as a whole.) The headteachers of the three schools eventually selected by the LEA all agreed to participate, and only then did members of the project team make direct contact with the headteachers of the schools concerned. For this first visit to the schools the tutors in charge of both the in-service and the adult education programmes went to meet the headteachers and describe the type of work which they hoped to do. The interviews were lengthy, interesting and cordial and the heads showed themselves to be receptive to the ideas of the project being developed within their school, although clearly some had more reservations than others.

At this stage, the paper referred to on p. 1, which set out the aims and objectives of the project and which was to serve as a basis for discussion with all concerned, was written and issued as *Paper I: The Aims of the Project*. This paper was circulated to the heads and staff of the three project schools at the beginning of the autumn term. A personal letter was then sent out from the tutor in charge of the teacher programme to all members of staff, containing details of the teacher in-service work proposed on the social dimensions of education, and the starting dates which had been agreed with the headteachers at each school. Finally, a tentative programme for the teacher groups was circulated to all three schools. This programme was not intended to be a final version but rather a series of suggestions to which members of staff could react. In the case of two schools this programme was accepted more or less in its entirety and was scheduled to continue up to half-term without alteration. As the work got under way, fairly radical proposals for the amendment of both the timing and the content of the programme were made by the teachers involved and this led to a reformulated programme for the second half of the term. This programme-flexibility was deemed an essential way of ensuring that teachers had a chance to help design their own work and thus became committed to it.

Experience in establishing the teacher in-service programme revealed the essential role of the headteacher in encouraging his staff to attend, and in emphasizing the importance of home–school relations. In the case of School 3, although a reasonable degree of success was ultimately achieved, there were initial difficulties arising from incomplete communication: while the headteacher then in post had agreed to participate actively in the research, it appeared that the staff concerned had not been made fully aware of the degree of commitment which participating in the project might involve for them. Thus, although everything had been arranged in all three schools in roughly the same way, the development of the project in School 3 was not altogether smooth and this led to a less successful programme within that school.

In School 3 we were eventually asked by the headteacher to meet the staff as a whole. In the event only the tutor in charge of the teacher programme was able to meet the staff and only a small proportion of the staff attended. The meeting was useful, but it must be said that the atmosphere was strained, members of staff feeling that they had been put in a position where they were committed to a project which they had been unable to discuss. During this meeting the headteacher made a proposal, which he had not made previously: that the project and its further work should be cleared by the parent–teacher association, which was very strong and well-organized in this school. This proposal was supported both by the staff present and by the in-service tutor for that school, and in addition a teacher liaison officer was elected from amongst the staff to arrange the future work of the in-service groups. However, attendance at such in-service meetings was throughout the project proportionately lower than in the other two schools.

In School 1 and School 2 the headteachers attended all sessions of the in-service programme, but in School 3 no in-service session provided by the project was ever attended by the headmaster.

At about the same time as the project was experiencing these difficulties at School 3 there were expressions of anxiety from one of the largest teachers' associations about the way the project might interfere with schools and teachers; it was also suggested that the project had been started without adequate consultation with teachers' organizations and school staff. It was clear that, in spite of our own efforts at consultation, we would now need to talk further with the branch secretary of this association, and a meeting between him and one of the project organizers was arranged. The branch secretary pointed out that some local members of the association were suspicious about certain kinds of educational research, especially if not cleared with them beforehand. He agreed that good home–school relations were important and gave a convincing account of his members' positive attitude towards improving them, but he thought that some of the aims of the project as expressed in the discussion document *Paper I* might well be misunderstood. The project organizer who had been invited left this meeting feeling that the branch secretary and his members were very much in favour of improving home–school relations through action-research programmes, provided they were established after the most thorough consultation. Further consultations then took place between the branch secretary and the two project directors, and the view was again expressed that research in schools should only proceed with the full support of the teachers and their professional organizations. As a general principle this view was, of course, fully accepted by the two directors. After a very full and frank exchange of views, this meeting concluded in an atmosphere of good faith and good humour. No further objections to the project were raised and no other teachers' organizations ever raised the matter with us. Offers were made to the teachers' organizations to provide one of the project organizers as a speaker at any of their meetings. This suggestion, however, was never taken up.

From our own perspective, therefore, it seemed that all reasonable effort had been made to communicate the aims and content of the research adequately to all concerned. The relevant organizations had been informed by letter as soon as the co-operation of the chief education officer had been obtained. But despite these efforts deeply-felt anxieties still persisted, arising from the view that much educational research is 'irrelevant' at the best, and a 'plundering of the schools to provide Ph.Ds' at the worst. All suspicions seem to have been allayed in the end, but the episode shows once again that action-research in such a sensitive area as home–school relations does demand painstaking consultation with all concerned well in advance of any start in the schools.

Meanwhile, the teacher programme at Schools 1 and 2 had already begun and was regularly attended by one quarter to one third of the staff in the two schools. The core attendance was of those who were particularly involved and/or interested in pastoral care. At School 3 the teacher programme had not yet begun, but the tutor in charge was invited to meet the executive committee of the parent–teacher association. During this meeting some reservations about the project were expressed. The headteacher, and the teacher-represent-ative of the PTA, criticized the commitment of time that the project would involve for members of staff and especially for married women teachers. The headteacher also criticized the inadequacy of the programme which was being proposed. He pointed out that only one session was to be given over to health education whereas at the same time a programme on health education had already been arranged by the local education authority; this programme, which consisted of a series of meetings throughout that first term, was being held in a central place and was available to all teachers in the city.

Later a further meeting with the PTA was organized and this was attended by both the teacher in-service tutor and the tutor in charge of the adult education programme for School 3. Finally, a compromise emerged. The adult education tutor was co-opted onto one of the sub-committees of the PTA, which was eventually convinced that the numbers of parents involved in the project's adult education programme would be very small, and that it was unlikely to compete with the regular PTA programme for parents. It was explained to the PTA that the aim was to attract those parents who did not usually attend school functions. At the time it appeared that on the parent side of the project the difficulties had been resolved, although it was eventually to prove that this was not the case. In the second term a time-table clash occurred between the functions of the PTA and those of our own adult education programme, which resulted in our being asked by the headmaster to cease our own parents' programme for that school. Most difficulties were, however, only temporary and did not directly affect the teacher side of the project. By mid-term all three schools were involved in the in-service programme, and in all three schools parents' groups had begun to develop their work.

In the case of the first two schools, which had started at the beginning of the term, the programme was well under way by half-term and teachers were expressing their appreciation of the work that was being done and their general satisfaction with the type of programme that had been offered and was being offered in the revised programme. There was criticism of the emphasis on films and videotape recordings, and a decision was taken that the programme in the second half of term should consist mainly of talks by visiting speakers, discussions, and seminars in which practical problems of the organization of school–community relationships would be discussed. There was sufficient support in all three schools for an ambitious programme of in-service work to be developed on Tuesday, Wednesday and Thursday of each week (one evening being given over to each school) and in general the work appeared to be satisfactory to the participants.

The experience gained by the researchers in establishing the teacher in-service courses and parent discussion groups revealed the paramount import-ance of consulting with all those individuals, groups and organizations affected and involved. In any sphere of human activity where changes are proposed, or discussed, which could alter habits, expectations, roles and well established patterns of behaviour, and where change can only be obtained through consent and democratic procedures, it is essential that consultations are thorough, wide and painstaking. This is as true in the field of home–school relations as it is in industry.

5 The three secondary schools

This chapter is devoted to a description of the three secondary schools, of their buildings and other facilities, and the catchment areas they serve. In order to give a general overview, simple statistical comparisons between the three project schools are included in this chapter (see Table 1), but we will begin with individual profiles of the schools.

School 1 is in an area of extensive council housing development which has grown up during the last twenty years. The original school buildings were opened in 1939 and further expanded in 1960. Since then more sections have been added, along with an assortment of temporary units to meet the expanding child population created by the large private and council housing estates which surround it. The LEA intends to expand the capacity of this secondary school from the existing size of nearly 700 pupils to a maximum of 900. The expanding child population of secondary school age is to be accommodated by building a new school within a short distance of School 1. So far the Department of Education and Science has refused two applications by the local education authority to build this new school. School 1, therefore, works under considerable pressure of pupil numbers and had a large number of applications from parents wishing to gain admission for their children. A vigorous and popular youth club is attached to the school and is used by the older pupils. The youth leader not only organizes the club but also teaches in the school and is responsible for making contact with parents and voluntary organizations.

Due to the long covered-way connecting the upper and lower schools, which were built as separate boys' and girls' schools at twenty-year intervals, and because of the assortment of huts, gymnasia, swimming pool and temporary buildings, the school can give a false impression of fragmentation to the casual visitor. The large school site of twenty-four acres with two main entrances, and its plethora of buildings, enable the school population to be dispersed, and this gives a general impression which seems to deny the existence of nearly 700 children aged between twelve and sixteen.

The school is bordered on one side, by a large pre-war housing estate of small and mainly semi-detached dwellings, and on the other sides by a large

Table 1 Comparisons between the three project schools (1972)

School	Number of pupils	Number of teachers (including full-time equivalents)	Teacher–pupil ratio	Teachers with deg-ree/Dip. Ed. (%)	Immigrant pupils* (%)	Pupils taking O levels in two final years (%)	Staying on in final year (%)	Receiving free meals (%)	Teachers aged 40 years & over (%)
School 1	672	49	1·14	20	0	19	46	8	47
School 2	442†	33	1·13	21	37	12	44	16	72
School 3	1003	57	1·17	32	0	32	52	6	42

* I.e. children born outside U.K.
† According to the headmaster, 30% of middle school output transferred to other secondary schools outside the catchment area.

Sources for table: obtained from the records of all three schools with permission of headmasters and co-operation of school office staff.

new council housing estate with the now familiar pattern of high-rise flats, semi-detached and modern terraced houses, old persons' bungalows and small family maisonettes. This council estate, the largest in the city, has been in a state of continuous development for over twenty years. It gives, to the socially aware and sensitive visitor, a feeling of brash, confident development, without a sense of community or continuity: it lacks that feeling of continuous human habitation which the ancient church and old pub can evoke. A few preserved, and now child-damaged, oaks survive among these houses to remind one that only a few years ago the estate was farmland. Many who live on the estate feel and express this lack of community and social awareness, but yet say how grateful they were to obtain a home there. Memories of homelessness and bad housing clearly offset the lack of community spirit and action. Because the houses were built by a council which has only recently come to recognize that council house tenants possess motor-cars, the narrow roads and pleasant wide grass verges are often covered in cars parked nose to tail.

The majority of families on this estate whose children attend secondary School 1 are skilled manual workers, although there is a substantial minority of people in lower white-collar occupations. Several large factories on the edge of the estate provide relatively well-paid shift-work for women, and many married women earn a second income for the family. The net effect gives the estate a character which can fairly be described as 'affluent working-class'. Overt signs of poverty are hard to find, yet under the surface they certainly exist.

The school does not have a formal parent–teacher association because the headmaster believes that it might become a 'caucus which is unrepresentative of parents as a whole' and would consist of 'seekers of special privileges for their own children'. Instead of a PTA, the school has encouraged the development of a school society open not only to parents, but to all members of what can loosely be called the local community. In addition, there is a local community association which has been attached to the school for many years and which has the right to use some accommodation within the school. This body has over 900 members who make extensive use of the school premises including the tennis courts and swimming pool. However, the community association appears to have little contact with parents on the estate.

School 1 had beyond doubt the most extensive and vigorous programme of events, and meetings aimed at encouraging parents to visit the school, of any of the three schools covered by this research. The attitudes of parents to these school initiatives are described in Chapter 10.

School 2 is dispersed over four separate and sub-standard buildings more than a mile apart and is situated in the old centre of the city. In almost every respect it is the least advantaged of all the secondary schools encountered by the project team in the city. It was, of course, selected for these characteristics in order to provide a contrast with the other two schools which had different and more privileged catchment areas. The school stands within an officially designated Educational Priority Area and is accepted by the Department of Education and Science as a 'school of exceptional difficulty'. Extra payments are made to the teachers and it has one of the best teacher–pupil ratios of any secondary school in the city. Despite these apparent advantages, however, in many respects it scores very poorly in comparison with the two other project schools, as Table 1 makes clear.

As mentioned, School 2 is divided between four different sites. The young pupils are housed in the main school building, where the headmaster has his office. This was constructed in 1931. The best accommodation which the school possesses was only acquired in 1973, as it had previously housed a college which had moved to a new building. The main site is extremely congested, with no playing fields, and is surrounded on two sides by huge prison-like walls over twenty feet high. All the open areas have 'temporary' huts and teaching units on them, giving the school a depressed, cramped appearance compared with the large fields and gardens of School 1. There is a small combined hall/gymnasium, but no school meals kitchen or dining room, and the library has been improvised in wooden huts.

The second site of the school is 500 yards away in a mid-nineteenth century building, taken over as a board school in 1876. It is used mainly for practical subjects and contains some sub-standard workshops and housecraft rooms. The building suffers from infestation with rats which the local authority has been unable to eliminate completely.

The third site is nearly one mile from the main school and occupies a building dating from 1878. It is depressing, damp and totally unsuitable for modern secondary education. In this most unsatisfactory setting a large number of children complete their final school years.

The last site of this fragmented school is based on a disused ambulance depot about half a mile from the main school. At this place a range of 'Newsom' activities, including motor engineering, sailing, rural studies and the keeping of livestock, is carried out. The site also serves as a social centre for older pupils, who have done a great deal to develop and maintain these facilities. It is fondly referred to as 'the farm'.

The physical separation of sites prevents a clear school identity from emerging in the minds of the pupils and teachers, resulting in considerable problems of co-ordination and communication, which inevitably sap teacher enthusiasm.

The school catchment area contains most of the slums and sub-standard houses in the city. As always they provide homes for the coloured immigrant population, the Irish, and the poor, as well as for the weak, inadequate and transient sections of the population. As these slums have been steadily cleared, modern high-rise flats and high-density housing have replaced them, but (apart from changing the appearance of the area) this has done little to alter the impression that the area is self-conscious of the fact that it houses the poorest and most disadvantaged people of the city. The school inevitably reflects the area and the people it serves.

Most of the coloured immigrant population has settled in this area of the city. They are mainly Indians, Pakistanis, West Indians and Ugandan or Kenyan Asians, who have taken over whole streets, including shops and places of entertainment, on which they have stamped their varied cultures. Most of the immigrants' children of secondary age attend School 2; this means that about thirty-seven per cent of the pupils in this school have immigrant parents. None of the other sixteen secondary schools in the city has anything even approaching this proportion of immigrant children, and the two other project schools have less than one per cent of immigrant pupils. Obviously, there are many social and cultural problems here which a few extra EPA resources do little to alleviate.

Many parents in the school catchment area are only too aware of the school's inadequacies, despite the valiant efforts of the staff, and they try to give their children a better chance by requesting a place in other secondary schools. The result of this in 1971–2 was that the parents of thirty per cent of all children leaving School 2's 'feeder' middle schools opted for other secondary schools. The headmaster, who provided this information, claimed that this was one of the most important causes of teacher frustration in the school. It was, he said, far more damaging than the severely adverse physical conditions in which the staff worked.

School 3 presents another contrast to School 2 and is a vivid reminder that different neighbourhoods give rise to very diverse comprehensive schools. This school had the largest number of pupils of any of the three project schools. Part of its catchment area contains some of the most attractive and expensive houses in the city, while another part includes a pre-war council house estate. In general it has the reputation of being a 'posh' school where the prosperous middle-class professional and business people like to send their children. The school also enjoys the reputation of being a school with a good academic record, a belief which is substantiated by examination statistics.

The site of ten acres on which School 3 is situated was purchased in 1938 although the separate boys' and girls' schools were not completed until 1962. In 1970 they were merged into a single co-educational secondary school; the separate buildings are connected by one incomplete covered way.

The pre-war council housing estate which is served by the school now has a somewhat battered appearance. Local evidence suggests that over the years this estate has lost many of its more able and higher-earning working-class families, as they have obtained housing transfers to more modern homes, with higher rents, on the new estates. These vacated homes have been taken up by less prosperous tenants from the city centre who have found it difficult to meet the higher rents of the new estates. This process has resulted in this part of the school's catchment area becoming representative of lower working-class socio-economic groups, including the elderly, and those with an inadequate head of family.

These two very different socio-economic housing areas existing cheek by jowl, sending their children to the same secondary school, produce a cross-section of pupils very different from the other two schools, with their relatively homogeneous intakes. This has produced social tensions not only between children, who in their early teens are often only too acutely aware of the social class structure of our society, but also amongst parents, whose often harsh opinions are recorded later in this report in the section dealing with the parent discussion-groups. The existence of such social diversity within the school has not resulted in a socially respresentative parent–teacher association; the PTA's active committee consists almost entirely of professional middle-class parents, and the level of academic success within the school correlates closely with social class.

The fact that it is one of the city's major further education centres distinguishes School 3 from the other two project schools. This centre is vigorous and well-used and means that adults already come into the school in large numbers as students in LEA adult education courses. Like the members of the PTA, these are mainly middle-class people, thus strengthening the middle-class ethos of the school.

It is now widely acknowledged that working-class parents, for a variety of reasons, make less contact with their child's school and teachers than do middle-class parents. The evidence from School 3 tends to suggest that where working-class parents believe themselves to be a minority in a predominantly middle-class catchment area, they not only withdraw from contact with the school but in many cases become antagonistic towards it. The antagonism extends, in this case, not only to the school but also to the PTA and its predominantly middle-class membership.

It is obvious that the three schools described above possess characteristics and levels of achievement which closely reflect the socio-economic status of the catchment area they serve. School 2 for example, is materially inadequate in almost every respect and it serves an area of indisputable social deprivation. On the other hand, School 3 is modern, enjoys social prestige and tops the league table of academic successes. It is no coincidence that its catchment area also contains many of the city's high-value houses and many parents of professional status. By comparison the head of School 2 could truly assert that not one of his children came from the home of professional parents.

It is of course a well-researched educational fact that secondary comprehensive schools vary considerably in a number of ways, and that they reflect the socio-economic status of the catchment area they serve. Our limited evidence supports existing research on this.

Before any action intended to improve home–school relations and community involvement in the school can take place, the history of the school, its internal organization, the level of academic achievement, staff and parent attitudes, and above all the social and economic characteristics of the catchment area need to be adequately researched. In 1970 a Schools Council report* on the education of socially disadvantaged children strongly recommended that schools should collect as much social information as possible about their catchment areas. Without some knowledge of these factors, unique to every school in the country, reference to any set of principles or techniques for improving home–school relations, and hence the education of children, seems doomed to failure.

It is thus hoped that this section, in addition to giving information about the schools involved in this project, may serve as a useful exemplification of the way in which a school catchment area can be described, and of the important social features which may be isolated and quantified. The use of questionnaires and interviews as methods of assembling vital social information about parents and community are described in Chapters 10 and 11.

---

* Schools Council Working Paper 27, *'Cross'd with adversity': the education of socially disadvantaged children in secondary schools* (Evans Methuen Educational, 1970).

6 Establishing the parents' meetings

It was intended that the parent groups should discuss the importance of the home, and the influences of both parents and the social environment on the education of the children. The programme was also scheduled to include information about modern developments in curriculum and teaching methods, and the changing structure of education. It was envisaged that several meetings would be devoted to discussing existing methods of communication between school and home, and to suggesting improved techniques for involving parents more in the everyday life of the school.

In addition, one of the major purposes of holding these meetings for parents was to discuss the views, attitudes and prejudices held by parents about the schools which their children attended, the teachers with whom they came into contact and the structure and aims of the formal education system as a whole. It was also intended to introduce to parents new ideas, such as that of the community school and home-visiting by teachers, and to observe their opinions and reactions. To reinforce the evidence collected at the parents' discussion meetings and the data from the questionnaires, an interview schedule was designed and used with a representative sample of parents to record attitudes and beliefs about relations between parents and teachers, and the home and the school.

Finally it was hoped to bring both teachers' and parents' groups together so that proposals for improving home–school relations could be discussed and acted upon. In this way some permanent impact of a practical nature might be made which could help to improve home–school relations at all three schools. In the event this was not realized in all cases and the reasons for this deficiency highlight the need for further research backed by more resources than were available to this limited pilot project.

The headteachers of the three project schools each agreed to help in securing a group of about fifteen parents living within the school catchment area. The schools at first suggested the names of well-known parents on whom they could rely to attend and help to organize school functions. But, as it was a fundamental aspect of the research that the views and attitudes of the non-participating parents were of the utmost interest and value, these suggestions were politely declined. This later caused difficulties at School 3, where the project's concern with the non-participating parent had the unintended result of giving the parent–teacher association the impression that its contribution to the life of the school had not been fully recognized.

Great care was taken to avoid the groups being self-selected from that small number of active, confident, articulate and inevitably middle-class parents who usually run PTAs and other activities which are intended to assist teachers and raise funds for the school. This does not ignore the valuable work done by PTAs but seeks to emphasize the fact that, apart from rare examples, the traditional PTA does not appear to have been instrumental in developing those close links between home and school which would create greater involvement of the community as a whole. This might not of course be attributable to PTAs in themselves, but rather to the fact that they can only operate effectively within the boundaries approved by headteachers and their staff. If there is to be greater parental involvement in schools, more trust in parents and in democratic principles will undoubtedly be required, as well as legislation to provide parents with a greater say in the governing of schools.

From the outset it was recognized that the traditional methods of adult education recruitment by way of formal posters, brochures on counters of public libraries, and advertisements in local newspapers, would not bring to the schools the non-participating parents. So it was decided to try other ways. One was to send out a small leaflet inviting parents to attend friendly, informal meetings where matters concerning the education of their children would be discussed. These leaflets were given to nearly all the children in the three schools in the hope that they would reach parents, but it is impossible to say how many actually reached the parents and were read by them. In addition, attractive informal posters advertising the meetings were displayed in local shops, post offices and launderettes. Probably the most effective method, however, was adopted by one of the parent-group tutors, who found the time to knock on the doors of parents living in the catchment area of School 3. As this difficult and skilled task was done during the day it resulted in attracting mainly housewives to the parent-group meetings.

The next step was to select three tutors who would each be responsible for one parent group. For School 1, on the large council estate, one of the project team, employed as a full-time tutor in the University Extra-Mural Department, undertook the task of organizing and running the parents' group. This tutor's teaching specialization lay in the field of industrial relations, but he also possessed a reasonable knowledge of schools and education through his membership of the City Council's Education Committee. His professional skill as an adult educator was also used when deciding the content of all three parent-group programmes and the teaching methods used.

For School 2, in the old part of the city centre, a practising school teacher, with an impressive record of voluntary effort in improving the provision of state education, was asked to take the parent discussion group. The fact that she taught in a primary school in School 3's catchment area gave her a unique knowledge of the area, schools and parents, but also placed her in a somewhat difficult position in relation to the headmaster and some of the staff of the school.

For School 3, with the predominantly middle-class catchment area, the services of a female professional research worker were secured. This group tutor had already participated in two major research projects, one for the Schools Council on the questions asked by very young children, and another assessing the work experience of sixth formers. The first project on children's curiosity was carried out in the catchment area of School 3 some time before the present project began. While the adult education experience of this tutor was limited, she had considerable expertise in the field of home interviewing and attitude assessment. Previous experience as an education social worker in east London, and as a teacher of handicapped children, provided a rich background for work with a project dealing with parental attitudes towards teachers and schools.

The three parent discussion groups began in October 1972, and were planned to run for ten consecutive meetings on one evening each week. A further series of six meetings was held after the Christmas break. Because it is widely believed that many non-participating parents lack confidence—no doubt stemming from their own school experience—when confronted by teachers on school premises, it was decided to hold the meetings on more 'neutral' ground. The parents at School 1 met in the youth club adjacent to the school; in School 2 meetings were held at first in an evening institute and later in the home of one of the parents; only at School 3 did the groups meet in the school because of the lack of suitable alternative accommodation. It is significant that the least successful parent meetings were at School 3, where the combination of school-based meetings and a strong PTA (which, as we have seen, had reservations about the project) seemed to undermine the efforts of the group tutor.

7 The parents' programme

On the first evening of the parent discussion meetings all three groups had sufficient numbers, and displayed enough vigour and interest, to become viable on a regular basis. The best attendances were at School 1 and the weakest at School 2. At the first meeting none of the traditional adult education rituals of enrolment, registers, syllabus, fees and student work expectation were gone through. The tutors merely explained why the meetings had been called and what part the discussion groups played in the research project as a whole. There was no precondition that group membership should depend on a promise of attendance at all ten meetings; the parents were merely invited to attend future meetings. The only charge made throughout the meetings was for coffee and biscuits. At the first two meetings the parents were asked no questions about their identity or motives for attending; every effort was made to produce informal, tension-free and friendly discussion groups where the tutors could observe, measure and record attitudes towards the school and the responses to suggestions for improving and changing home–school relations. By the third meeting the tutors had gained the confidence of the groups sufficiently to obtain personal details from the parents and to present a modest outline of the ground to be covered at future meetings.

The largest of the three parent groups (School 1) contained only sixteen people and the smallest (School 2) fourteen. School 3, with a child population of just over 1000 and an active PTA, was able to recruit only fifteen parents. While these modest numbers were good from an action-research point of view, in that attitudes and opinions could be probed better in a small intimate group than in a large, more formal, gathering, the numbers were disappointing from the point of view of parental interest and involvement. Yet the evidence of the interviews held later with parents suggests that parents have, none the less, a strong interest in the school and in their child's education. It is of crucial importance that the ability and inclination of parents to attend experimental discussion meetings established with the minimum of resources should not be taken as a definitive measure of parental interest in home–school relations. Much work and experiment needs to be carried out, aimed not only at establishing the best methods of attracting parents to meetings dealing with many aspects of education, but also at determining the best ways of communicating this information in an interesting and stimulating way. It should be recognized that formal parent-education, if that unattractive description must be used, will probably never attract more than a minority of parents, but that if the right techniques can be developed such education could nevertheless become the basis upon which wider home–school relations might be built. The evidence collected from three small parent discussion groups cannot in any way provide definitive answers but it can perhaps suggest some of the more promising lines to be explored.

The choice of group tutors who had no formal connection with the schools, and the holding of the meetings on 'neutral' premises in an informal atmosphere, was intended to eliminate teacher/school domination and to raise the confidence of parents. It was also vital from the outset to make it clear that the fund-raising and social-support role of the conventional PTA fell far short of the project workers' conception of good home–school relations. This value judgement, which is an essential part of action-research, was communicated firmly to the parents. The tutors made it clear that they supported much more radical views of parent involvement, including parental participation as ancillary support in selected teaching situations, along with a much greater use by the community of school facilities as of right.

Before the meetings began the three tutors met on several occasions to determine the main topics to be included, the use of teaching aids and the way in which the discussions would be guided towards consideration of existing techniques for involving parents in school activities, and the way improvements and innovations could be made. All three tutors were to keep observational records of the way their meetings progressed. The production of a brief syllabus, to be introduced to the parents in each group after the second week, was left to the individual tutor after certain broad guidelines had been agreed.

The use of films,* videotapes, tape recordings and other teaching aids, along with the choice of specialist visiting speakers and other teaching methods was left in the hands of the individual tutors, as was the question of visits to other schools and educational institutions. For example, one group visited a middle school in another part of the city where the headmaster played host.

Certain essential key topics were discussed at all three parent-group meetings and these included:

(a) How young children learn, and how new teaching methods and curricula have developed and changed since most of the parents in the groups were at school.

* A brief list of films and where to obtain them is given in Appendix VII.

(b) The influence and importance of the home, family, parents, language, social class and the community environment on the mental and intellectual development of the young child at school.

(c) The aims of modern secondary education, integrated studies, modern maths and English, and the preparation of the child for examinations, jobs and entry into higher education.

(d) The educational importance of home–school relations; the attitude of parents to teachers and vice versa, and the role of the school in the community it serves.

(e) The traditional techniques used to develop links between home and school, and the role of institutions such as PTAs, along with an examination of new and often radical ways of improving links between parents and teachers.

Group discussion under the gentle guidance and control of the group tutor was the method used to get the parents to think about these topics and to disclose their feelings, opinions, prejudices and attitudes. The standard method was for the tutor to introduce the topic, for example the influence of social class upon the child's attitude to school and learning, which would be followed in some cases by a short film or videotape, after which the discussion would begin. In the case of a visiting specialist speaker the tutor would act as chairman as well as helping to stimulate the discussion.

The advantages of this method in the sphere of non-vocational liberal adult education are well known, but worthy of mention nevertheless. Firstly, the method is one of the most acceptable ways of probing, with a group of people possessing diverse views and strong prejudices, some of the most controversial of social topics—and education often falls under that description. Provided the tutor gives a balanced account of the arguments for and against, and lays down firm but fair guidelines for the discussion to follow, people respond in a way which enables vigorous and stimulating discussion to take place without acrimony. Secondly, it usually encourages people to state their views, however unpopular, without the rancour and unpleasantness which accompany the unstructured argument, and this proved an invaluable method of recording deeply held beliefs. Finally, once the discussion is in full swing this method enables the tutor to introduce new material which fits logically into the discussion and which also extends the line of thought being pursued. Such new material is often difficult to introduce when the group is 'cold'. An example of this last point was the introduction, into a discussion on how much teachers should tell parents about what their children are being taught, of the radical view that parents should be able to participate in some teaching situations with their children. When deliberately introduced by the tutor in this planned way, a valuable discussion by ordinary parents developed which other techniques, such as using interviews or questionnaires, would probably not have elicited. Unfortunately, due to the obvious difficulty of using a tape recorder, these discussions could only be assessed by the tutor after the parents had gone home.

The visiting specialist speakers invited by the tutors to talk to the groups proved, in general, a quite successful method of evoking responses. The educational professionals who proved of most interest to the parents were education welfare officers, unattached community workers, headteachers, and the teachers who explained to parents the mysteries of modern maths and integrated studies. It must be made clear, however, that such speakers some-times had an inhibiting effect upon the parents, who felt that they lacked sufficient knowledge to probe with confidence the social value of the work done by these professional people. The best discussions took place after the speaker had left and the group felt more relaxed and able to discuss the talk with the tutor they had grown accustomed to. The greatest interest was expressed about the work of the education welfare officers, and the value of curricular innovations such as integrated studies. Many parents expressed the view that their own education had lacked the stimulus and breadth which modern teaching methods apparently provided. One tutor and his group felt strongly that if integrated studies projects could include parental involvement, the parents and children would find a common point of contact which would bring home and school much closer together.

Generally speaking, visual aids such as films and videotapes proved less stimulating and useful than group discussion following a talk or demonstra-tion. BBC videotapes such as *Parents and Teachers, Counselling and Guidance* and *Test for Life* were used. They aroused varying degrees of approval, and comments such as 'interesting' and 'it was never like that when we were at school' followed. But, perhaps because of the conditioning effect of the one-way communication provided by television, the videotapes did not evoke vivid responses and the uncovering of prejudices to the same extent as the carefully structured if apparently casual group discussion method.

Inevitably, many of the parents attending the discussion groups at all three schools belonged to that category of parents who can be described as showing an active, if largely uninformed, interest in their children's education. More precise evidence of how limited or extensive this interest was is not available, because the tutors sensed that any attempt to cross-examine parents about these delicate matters in such a short period would prove detrimental to the existence of the discussion groups. It was also felt that if the parents were asked how much interest they had in the school and their child's education they would be bound to exaggerate because of the stress the tutors had already given to the importance of such attitudes.

During the sessions in which the three tutors met to discuss the progress of the parent discussion groups, it was agreed that if parents had a poor record of contact with the school it was unlikely that they would take the trouble to join and attend evening discussion groups. However, it was patently clear that where the tutors had undertaken the difficult task of knocking on the doors of parents about whom the school knew little it was possible to attract these non-participating parents to the meetings. Evidence to date suggests that if parent discussion groups could be held during the day, with facilities available for the care of very young children, it is possible to get many house-wives to attend with whom, mainly for domestic reasons, the school finds it difficult to communicate. About one quarter of the parents attending the groups could be described as having a record of limited contact with the school which their child attended. Another quarter were parents fairly well known to the school and on whom the school could nearly always rely to attend meetings and other functions held for parents. The remainder were average parents who did not lay great importance on close contact with the school because they thought the school was doing a reasonable job without them. Many parents in this majority found it difficult to accept the view that home is at least as important as school in their child's education.

So far we have only described the way in which the parent groups were established, how they operated the programme, and the teaching methods employed. In the next chapter, the parent-group tutors who ran the meetings at School 2 and School 3 respectively give a subjective description of the way they conducted the discussions, the parents they attracted to the meetings, and the opinions, fears and attitudes expressed about schools and teachers.

8 The parents' discussions: reports from group leaders

School 2

'School 2 is right on the edge of the catchment area, with no housing in the immediate vicinity. The catchment area is divided up into parcels of housing by main roads, shopping centres, the railway, parks and waste plots. The headmaster described the school as serving seven separate villages. It is an area of mixed urban renewal and decay. There are high-rise flats, medium-rise flats and old terraced houses. It is an area of demolition and rebuilding. When we came to interview parents in the area, two houses in our small sample of twenty addresses had been demolished. This of course adds greatly to the school's problems. It causes genuine concern to many parents and is often given as a reason why parents wish their child to attend another secondary school. This is not the place to go into the physical provision of the school in greater detail (Chapter 5), except perhaps to say that inadequate provision lower teacher and parent morale, unless there is a determined effort to overcome it. The fact that this school has only one hall, which is also used as a dining room and a gymnasium, is not only limiting to daily school life, but also makes it that much more difficult to provide a welcoming atmosphere for parents. In contrast, the other schools in the project, both being the result of the amalgamation of two single-sex schools on adjoining sites, have two halls, two dining rooms, two gymnasia—and a swimming pool each! Buildings are not of vital importance in home–school relations, as many of the Educational Priority Area projects have shown, but position and design can help or hinder innovations.

'It was decided not to hold the parents' discussion group meetings in the school as we were particularly interested in recruiting those who went 'unwillingly to school''. The split nature of the catchment area made it difficult, however, to find a suitable centre and this was a problem that was never fully resolved. I held the meetings up till Christmas break in the nearby technical college and then moved to the library or reading room in the local central evening institute, finishing up with the last two meetings in the house of one of the members of the group. I feel another attempt at involving parents in discussion would do better to start with a smaller area—one of the headmaster's "villages". As it was, because most of the group came from one area, they wanted to retreat to it; I, committed to a wider involvement, did not feel able to do so until those last two meetings. Then the experience of meeting in a private house made me feel that we had reached an excellent starting point, a possible growing point—just as the meetings came to an end.

'But physical and geographical difficulties are not the only problem in the way of parent attendance at meetings. This is an area where many immigrant families live, where many work long hours. In some families, when father arrives home, mother goes out to an evening job. Shift work is common. Fathers are away on the boats, or just away, and there is no one to look after the children. More women have more children than in other areas and have not the time or energy left for evening meetings. "Baby-sitting" is less acceptable among workers, and is often not even considered in an area such as this. Added to this there is nervousness about walking the streets in the dark. In such an area great flexibility and imagination on the part of the school will be needed to encourage fruitful home–school relations. In the words of the headmaster of School 2:

The school is not situated in the centre of the community, but is tucked away in an uninhabited corner of it. It is not an easy school for parents to get to. Open days have been declared on which parents might come to the school and walk around and visit classrooms. The response was practically nil. The school formed a parent association in 1967. This ceased to function after three years through lack of support.

In view of this situation the initial method of publicizing the parents' discussion groups through the schools was unlikely to gain much response.

'This method, however, had been decided upon as the main channel of communication for all three schools. We endeavoured to reach all parents by keeping notices as simple and welcoming as possible. I visited headteachers in the area asking for their co-operation in encouraging parents to come along. I doubted the power of the written word in this situation, and hoped some personal encouragement might be forthcoming. However, I have no evidence that anyone connected with the schools did more than hand the notices to the children to take home. I placed posters in shops, churches and a club, and, as the meetings continued, further posters advertising particular topics, films or speakers. As I had suspected, however, it needed personal invitations to encourage people to come along. One mother and one married couple came as a result of the notice from school; no one as the result of seeing a poster. Four more came after I had written them a letter: two of these four I already knew, the other two names I had suggested to me. Another seven came as the result of a face-to-face invitation and two were brought in for the last two meetings by the woman in whose house we met.

'Faced with the problem of recruiting again in this area for an educational discussion group, I think it might be wiser to arrange for social contact first, or to concentrate on a more limited neighbourhood, so that people could meet near their home. I should like to try meeting in the houses of various members of the group, each host or hostess being partly responsible, along with the group leaders, for canvassing support for the meeting at his or her house. This pattern might seem to emphasize the social rather than the educational nature of such meetings but I should like to submit that this view would be to see a false polarity in the situation. My experience as parent-group leader convinced me that the social aspect of our meetings was as important as the more narrowly educational. For it is not only information which many parents need to help them play a more constructive role, but with it a chance to grow in confidence, to find out that they do have an opinion and that people will listen to it. Social contact is for most people an important, if not vital, element in gaining confidence in themselves and their own opinions.

'Eventually there were sixteen members of the group, but, as has already been seen, two of them were only recruited for the last two meetings. There were never more than nine at any one meeting, numbers dropped to three on one occasion, and the normal attendance was six to eight. The inability to recruit more widely must be considered disappointing, but the enthusiasm generated by the group and their obvious enjoyment convinced me that there must be many potential candidates for informal adult education in this area. Given some time and resourcefulness, it should be possible to reach them. This opinion was later reinforced when I visited several homes in the area to interview the families, and found them not only ready to talk but obviously pleased to become involved in thinking about schools and education.

'It will be obvious from what I have already said about recruitment to the group, and perhaps from what one might expect of this method of organization, that the group was, by its self-selected nature, unrepresentative of parents in the inner-city area. I wish to make it clear that we never, at any time, imagined that we were speaking for all parents in the neighbourhood, even when our group was unanimous in attitude or conviction. But this having been freely admitted, it must be emphasized that no one in the group had ever attended an adult education class before, and to meet weekly to talk, discuss and learn was a new experience. We were sounding out opinion and attitudes among people never before reached in this way.

'We did have with us men and women born in the area, whose parents went to school in the area, but one of the group's most obvious characteristics was the high proportion of those who had moved in from other countries. We had mothers from Spain, Malta, India, Fiji, the Canary Islands and Ireland. Four of them had marked difficulty with the English language, but, far from detracting from their pleasure in the meeting, this seemed to add another dimension, and they took pride in their new-found ability to express their thoughts. This was particularly noticeable with one woman, who at first only spoke when she felt very strongly about something and apologized for her English every other sentence. Gradually this changed and when the second series started after Christmas she was talking much more freely and confidently, although still sometimes surprising herself. Perhaps the fact that she had been interviewed on local radio about the meetings helped!

'Much of these parents' determination to see their children benefit from education was fired by the feeling that they themselves missed out in some way and were leading unnecessarily restricted lives as a result. The most extreme example of this was probably a woman whose schooling in Malta virtually ended at the age of nine with the coming of the war. When schools reopened she was almost fourteen; she went back for two or three months, but by then her mother was dying and she was needed at home. She is determined that her children shall avail themselves of every educational opportunity possible.

'This sense of the lack of education limiting their lives in some cases extended, of course, to their husbands. As one woman said:

He is a waiter. Nothing wrong with that. It is all right to be a waiter. But when you are fifty-five and still a waiter! I want something better for my son.

Differences in experience and outlook of course there were, but all were united in the belief that education was of crucial importance. It was seen as important in getting a job and therefore securing a pleasant and rewarding life-style. They also saw education as giving confidence and a social ease, qualities which they felt they themselves lacked. Indeed, at times they seemed to have an almost frightening belief in the power of education to solve all the individual's problems.

'Those who had been brought up in the area felt that schools had changed so much since "their day" that there was a whole new situation to learn about; while those who had not themselves been brought up in this country felt that they must learn as much as they could for the sake of their children. They were all very ready to talk of their own school days, and felt that their children were enjoying a much better education. When we discussed the wider aspects of childhood, again there was agreement within the group, but to the effect that, outside school, life had grown more cramped and narrow for their children than it had been for them. They remembered the countryside, or almost traffic-free streets to play in, and agreed that they had enjoyed a physical freedom, a freedom to roam, denied to their children. They also remembered their parents having more friends where, as children, they could drop in at any time, be looked after, be fed. Their own children had a more restricted social life. They talked of isolation, living in little boxes, the need to be reassured by exchanging experiences.

'As a counter to all this there was high praise for the nursery class. Again and again over the weeks they returned to how much their children had enjoyed the experience and had gained from it, and how much they too had learned from their children going there. They were conscious of how helpful it had been to them personally to meet and talk with other mothers.

'They were firm supporters of open-days, fêtes and almost any activity the school wished to put on, and all felt that easy communication between themselves and teachers, when it existed, did much to dispel misunderstanding. When it did not exist, there was much anxiety, resentment and suspicion.

'They welcomed the chance of an informal chat, and those whose children had newly moved to secondary schools felt the lack of opportunity for casual contact. They were encouraged by the others to take their worries to school rather than nurse them at home. I was surprised by the enthusiasm with which they welcomed the idea of home-visiting by teachers. As one man said: 'I can never talk in a hall or school classroom. I can say what I think in my own sitting-room.' There were no dissenters.

'The group generated a great deal of lively enjoyment and surprised visitors by the freedom with which the parents "chipped in" and showed readiness to relate to their own experience the points made. Perhaps this last circumstance could be taken as evidence that their thinking and use of language was, to use Bernstein's phrase, 'context-bound'. This being so, the meetings were, I feel, most useful not only in encouraging the expression and formulation of thoughts and feelings, but also in introducing a more "universalistic" approach. The parents enjoyed going by minibus to visit another school, looking at books brought by the children's librarian, or at slides and films—and always talking, differing, agreeing.

'They were a small group, however, almost all invited personally. Perhaps discussion-group membership in a neighbourhood such as this will only grow from such a beginning. Perhaps people must be contacted on their own doorstep or meeting places, in shops, pubs, launderettes or school playgrounds or classrooms. The school has much to gain from closer contact with parents. I believe it is also in the best position to make that contact. True, there are long-standing prejudices and fears to be overcome, but the school has a place in the community, a base to work from; and parental interest in the child can create a positive link and give extra weight and purpose to the relationship.

'Adults winkled out of their tele-viewing homes, made more confident by the acquisition of information and, more importantly, the experience of expressing their ideas and having them taken seriously, are more likely to be ready to contribute to fuller understanding between parents and teachers.'

School 3

'As School 3 served socially differing neighbourhoods it was hoped to recruit a socially representative group of parents. Three methods of recruiting were adopted. They were as follows:

1 Notices about the discussion group were displayed in local shops (the library declined to display a notice).
2 Parents of first-year pupils were circularized through the school.
3 Direct approaches were made to parents on doorsteps and in the streets near the school.

Particular efforts were made to recruit parents in the immediate neighbourhood of the school, which consisted mainly of a pre-war council housing estate. A high proportion of the women approached worked part-time; several mothers expressed interest but said they could not go out and leave the children in the evenings if husbands were working overtime or on shifts. A few were too shy ("I wouldn't dare say anything") and one was hostile—"I've gotta go to work haven't I? To pay for all the things she needs at that bloody school!"

'Attendance was lower than anticipated. Fears of an overwhelming preponderance of articulate middle-class parents swamping discussions were not fulfilled. Fifteen parents attended one or more meetings of the group, but weekly attendance fluctuated between nine and two. In terms of social class, nine parents could be regarded as middle-class and six as working-class. More women (ten) attended than men (five). Most parents had children in the middle and/or secondary schools but a few had children above and below this age range.

'Commitment to regular weekly attendances had not been stressed during recruitment, but parents were told that meetings would be held each Thursday at 7.30 p.m., and they were encouraged to come along as often as possible. The meetings were held in a classroom in the school. Regularity of attendance appeared to be affected by bad weather, work, illness and domestic commitment. Nine meetings were held, incorporating a programme of films, speakers and discussion, as follows:

1 Introduction to the project, followed by general discussion of educational topics and personal experiences and opinions.
2 Film—*Learning by Doing*; discussion of objectives and methods of primary education.
3 Drugs. The group attended a meeting about drug abuse organized by the PTA. Points raised were discussed in later meetings.
4 'Relationships between teachers and parents in primary schools.' A former college of education lecturer (now engaged in research) spoke of the need for co-operation between parents and teachers, and during the discussion that followed suggested ways in which parents could help their children.
5 *Parents and Teachers*, a videotape recording of the BBC RoSLA programme; discussion of the community school and consideration of ways in which parental interest could be expressed when children were at secondary school.

6 Film—*Aims in Secondary Education*; the headmaster of School 3 attended this meeting and joined in discussion after the film. He answered questions and provided explanations of both general and particular matters relating to the school and to the opportunities for pupils when they left school.
7 The raising of the school leaving age. The year mistress for the first full year at School 3 to be affected by RoSLA described curricula planned for these pupils and discussed practical problems.
8 Language and communication. Parents were invited to bring along examples of questions asked by their children. These were used to illustrate patterns of communication between children and adults. The importance of communication was considered both in relation to learning to speak in infancy, and to discussing problems of adolescence.
9 School governors. A governor of School 3 described the functions and influence of school governors and managers, and explained their part in the administration of education in the ctiy.

'The discussions were informal and generally amicable. They tended to follow a fluctuating course, narrowing to personal anecdotes and expanding to more abstract educational topics. Discussions were, of course, affected by differences in personality and outlook—one member of the group, for example, tended to self-reference any matter being discussed, while another tended to intellectualize. Wherever possible, personal experiences, opinions and grievances were used to illustrate wider issues; problems raised were looked at from different points of view—those of parent, child, teacher or employer—and insights were gained into possible reasons for other people's perplexing behaviour and attitudes. The parents' interest in education tended to be focused on the schools their children attended and they appeared to be most interested in the specific stage of schooling their children had reached.

'The provision of a film or speaker provided a focal point for discussion and questions. Speakers seemed to be more popular, as they could be questioned and argued with, while films were always criticized for shortcomings in content or lack of relevance; nevertheless, the latter provided a useful stimulant to discussion, and a shared experience on which to base arguments. There were widely differing views among even such a small group of parents, and the meetings were quite lively with almost everybody participating, apparently welcoming the opportunity to express opinions and air grievances without actually making complaints.

'Sometimes differences in outlook and life experience made discussion difficult as different parents preferred to conduct discussion at different levels, often reflecting educational background. Some parents may have felt inferior in the face of articulate academic discourses, while others no doubt felt irritated by lengthy personal reminiscences.

'There was some evidence of polarity of parental attitudes which was expressed in terms of social class. Locational references were made by the parents themselves to the names of well-known but different housing areas; these implied categorizations of social class and academic ability, as well as language and behaviour. Within such a small group it was possible to explore such attitudes and consider whether perceptions of stereotypes were really true. The assertion that middle-class parents "want to organize and do everything their way, and run the show", making working-class parents feel their contribution was inferior, was modified in discussion to agreement that they weren't *all* like that, but that a few did tend to dominate, and sometimes discouraged working-class support for parents' activities in connection with school. Appreciation was expressed of the efforts of a middle school headteacher to encourage working-class interest and support. His control of all parents' activities within the school ensured that the middle-class did not dominate, and the high attendance at a recent open evening was attributed to his observable fairness and determination that no one section of parents or children received preferential attention. It was suggested that working-class parents in the area recognized his efforts—"he treats us all the same"—but it also emerged that this policy had antagonized some middle-class parents, particularly those who favoured streaming. Middle-class parents in the group tended to be in favour of streaming as they thought it was a more efficient way of teaching and they felt their children benefited from such a system; worries were expressed about disruptive children in a class distracting a teacher's time and attention away from more reserved children who wanted to work. The working-class parents, however, felt that mixing children up helped them to get on with all sorts of people and prevented certain groups from looking down on other groups in a superior way.

'Speech and behaviour were also discussed: it was stated, for example, that teachers preferred the children to talk "posh". "But if they get into bad habits and don't talk properly how are they ever going to learn to spell properly?" It was suggested that teachers recognized differences in speech and categorized children accordingly; this tended to make working-class parents rather defensive about their speech and sometimes inhibited them from speaking to teachers.

'But responsibility for the behaviour of children was usually placed squarely on the parents, and strong criticism was expressed of parents who did not correct their children's bad language. An interesting discussion occurred about "bad families". If there is a "bad family" in your road what should you do? If you let your children play with their children they will probably pick up bad language and habits. If you try to offer friendship to the family your other friends may criticize or drop you. The examples mentioned illustrated the dilemma of parents who try to maintain what they regard as proper standards for their children, and the inevitable tendency to reject those who fall below such standards. Discussion of what could be done to help families with low standards brought out some resentment about the amount of "welfare" assistance such families seemed to get, and the opinion that they would be unlikely to be accepted in the community until they mended their ways.'

9 The teacher in-service groups

This chapter describes the way in which the teacher groups were established, and the experience of working with them and evaluating them. Whilst it is prudent, in view of the small-scale nature of the project, to emphasize once again that the work sought to come to terms with possibilities and to test conjectures rather than to establish incontrovertible facts, there were certain major elements of the teacher in-service commitment which should be described in some detail.

To begin with, it was difficult to design the type of course which would attempt to develop further the teachers' social awareness, whilst at the same time providing a series of experiences which would be more immediately meaningful and attractive to them. In addition, the need to persuade teachers of their own role in course-design, and in the definition of their own needs in particular, was of paramount importance if the project team were to identify the teachers' needs correctly. All the teachers concerned had extensive experience of previous in-service courses where the objectives in terms of content were fairly well-defined and laid down for them. Our task was different but no less important. We were asking the teachers to be explorers and definers of new and unfamiliar areas, and at the same time we were encouraging them to participate in experiences, such as a group critique of their own activities, which would inevitably lead to feelings of insecurity on their part. Thus the design of the in-service programme was highly experimental, and a compromise had to be struck between the demands of the teachers for knowledge (for example, about the organization of the social services department of the local authority) and the need to build in new experiences as a way of acquiring greater social awareness.

The assumption at the outset was that if teachers and parents were to work more closely together there would be a need for sensitivity and understanding on our part in approaching the schools to offer concrete support, both human and financial. In the search for better home–school relations only minimal support, either from the community at large or from institutions of teacher education, seemed to have been previously available to teachers. It was, therefore, the purpose of the teachers' groups to attempt to come to terms with some of the theoretical and practical implications of the development of a greater community commitment to education. The intention was to help teachers to consider how they might need to change their roles, how support for this change might be achieved, and to what extent the changes necessitated extra support from outside resources.

The programme of in-service education was offered to all three schools on an individual-school basis and each course was to a great extent designed by the members of staff within those schools. After the run-up period of the first half term, teachers played the main part in designing the programme, and in determining the frequency of meetings and the content and organization of those meetings. The university School of Education supported their efforts by putting at their disposal its organization, some of its in-service finances, and in the early stages an in-service tutor.

A fairly close role-description was evolved for the teacher-group leader. He would, for example, be expected to have an acquaintance with the overall aims of the programme, so that he could answer general questions about it and know where to refer more specific ones. It was envisaged that it would be his task to liaise closely with the headteacher and staff, to study the programme schedules provided and to use these as guidance for the discussion. He would be expected to initiate discussions within the teacher group and be sensitive to its members' professional needs. The introduction of visiting speakers, and the arrangements for payment both of the speakers and for the film and video-tape recordings which were shown in the early part of the programme—all these were his responsibility. In addition, it was hoped that, where applicable, relevant visits would be arranged by him. To assist in the assessment of progress, he would be expected to draw up a report after each meeting about what had happened and the issues that had been raised. Finally, he had to help the group begin to plan its own activities and commence a study of the school in its social context. From the beginning, it was intended that he would withdraw from involvement in the development work of that group as time progressed, whilst remaining available for consultation and discussion. The skill of the teacher-group leader in achieving a balance between non-directive and programmed activity was indispensable, for it was considered important for teachers to feel that the sessions were worthwhile—in that they were learning something of use to them—while at the same time there was to be within their hands an important element of self-direction. Thus, a detailed yet flexible programme was published in advance, from which basis it was hoped that the teachers would realize the options open to them in the development of the work of the group.

The function of the teacher groups in the project was clearly laid down and their objectives made available to participating schools. It was hoped that the groups would work to develop increased awareness of the social dimensions of learning, of the teacher's role and of the relationship between the social and educational services. It was clear that, in pursuing the development of an interest in community involvement, the groups would have to seek to come to terms with different value systems in a pluralist society. Finally, it was envisaged that the work might encourage teachers to begin to develop action-research into their school and its context.

It will be recalled that the three schools had originally been chosen in order to provide a broad social spread. In addition to differences in catchment area, there were also variations in size and staffing (see Table 2). Each school had

Table 2 The staff of the schools by staffing provision, age range and qualifications (1972)

	School 1	School 2	School 3
Staffing provision:			
No. of full-time staff	44	31	49
No. of part-time staff*	9(5)	3(2·1)	13(8·3)
Staff–pupil ratio†	1:14	1:13	1:17
Age range:			
20–4	9	1	7
25–9	9	5	6
30–4	6	2	10
35–9	4	2	15
40–4	6	5	5
45–9	3	5	7
50–4	3	5	4
55–9	8	6	5
60+	5	3	3
Qualifications:			
M.A.	—	1	1
B.A.	4	2	13
B.Sc.	3	4	3
Dip. Ed. or equivalent	3	—	1

* Full-time equivalent (in terms of half-days worked) shown in brackets.
† Pupil–teacher ratio calculated from numbers of full-time and full-time equivalent staff.

a different system of pastoral care, different methods of seeking to develop home–school relations, and significantly different levels of contact and degrees of satisfaction with the back-up social and welfare services. It was therefore to be expected that each staff group would have different professional needs, and that this fact would need to be reflected in the work of the teacher groups.

For these reasons, one programme would probably not have been adequate for all three schools. None the less, the problem of the setting-up of the teachers' programme was made easier by the fact that the same tutor was responsible for the work of all three groups. Thus, in spite of the different programmes which emerged in each of the three schools, the work of the three groups had certain common strands. They had in common, for example, a search for information about the relationships between the social and educational services, and an examination of what a greater community involvement in education might mean in terms of how the roles of the teachers in the school concerned might need to change.

The initiative to establish the teachers' groups in the three schools was taken through the headteachers. Letters were distributed to all members of staff, and headteachers were given copies of *Paper I: The Aims of the Project* and the parents' questionnaire, to distribute to colleagues for information. In addition, a draft programme of in-service work was sent to all staff for criticism and comment prior to the start of the programme. Two of the schools immediately took up the offer of help in preparing a programme more closely tailored to their needs, and were quickly able to define their own requirements in this area of work. School 3, because of the problems we described in Chapter 4, did not follow until later. The programmes for each school were made available to the other schools, in order that a cross-fertilization of ideas with regard to the type of work which might be appropriate could be developed, rather than as an attempt to achieve uniformity.

In Schools 1 and 2, where an early start was made, attendances were very good from the beginning, with between one quarter and one third of the staffs of each school taking part on each occasion, and with a nucleus of six to eight staff who participated on every occasion. In these two schools the headteachers were able to be present at every meeting and the deputy head also attended on most evenings. In addition, the groups benefited immensely from the participation and expertise of the education welfare officer (EWO) who attended on many occasions. The chief education welfare officer visited each of the schools, including the one which started its programme rather later, and took part in many of the discussions, attending a large number of the sessions at the inner-city school (School 2). The participation of EWOs, and later of other members of social services departments, turned out to be an important element in the success of the work. It was apparent that teachers who were responsible for pastoral care in the school, regardless of whether this was part of a well-defined but separate system or one based upon an integrated year-group organization, relied heavily upon the skill of the education welfare officer—for example, in contacting homes and detecting truancy. A comparison of the teacher's and EWO's conception of an orientation to a child's problems was thus important in co-ordinating any help which was to be given.

Underlying the decision about the school-based nature of the projected work was a major problem which had been encountered in previous work of this kind with groups of teachers from different schools, namely that discussions had often failed to capture the essence of the problem because the school's organization and the way in which this was linked with the functions of other social service agencies had been discussed, of necessity, away from concrete examples and at far too abstract a level. Because members of staff had been withdrawn from their individual schools to talk in teachers' centres, in the School of Education, or in colleges, about problems that were not specific to their day-to-day experience, the discussions proceeded at one remove, as it were. From this earlier experience it was clear that each of these schools would have its own problems and thus, despite their many common ties, it was necessary for each school to have its own in-service programme. At the preliminary meeting in each school, draft programmes of work were put forward for discussion and observations about the future development of work. In each school the programme was subjected to substantial and critical revision, and at two schools this resulted in self-programming work emerging.

Initially the group meetings took the form of seminar discussions of film or videotape-recorded material. Sometimes the work involved a commonsense discussion of a case-study or of principles, either with regard to the school's pastoral organization or to the organization of the project. Questions of parental involvement were raised quite freely and discussion ranged over a wide variety of ways of involving parents. Many of these ways, such as the possibility of parents being able to sit in on lessons, were discussed sympathetically, though often immense practical difficulties stood in the way of their implementation. And later, when on other occasions the groups heard a talk by a visiting speaker from one of the social services departments, the police and probation service, the Churches, the education welfare service, the school health service and so on, there was always time to build on the initial momentum through discussion and argument. Attempts were made to draw into the school, at times and places convenient to a large number of teachers, professionals who worked side by side with teachers who worked in that school, but who were often unacknowledged and perhaps even unknown to them. The teachers were then invited to discuss matters of common interest and the way in which their roles might interlink with those of other professional colleagues.

In addition to these opportunities, seminars where a visiting speaker came to discuss in detail some particular organization or piece of legislation provided a variety of insights and points of view. In this respect the talks by the chief education welfare officer were well received. Material was available in draft form from the (at the time) forthcoming Ralphs Report,* and the extensive description of the functions of the EWO from that document proved particularly useful in stimulating discussion. Another successful and much appreciated visit was that of the police juvenile liaison officer. There was great interest in his work and not a little admiration of his knowledge of the

---

* Recommendations summarized in *The Training of Education Welfare Officers— Training Document No. 19* (Luton: Local Government Training Board, 1974).

law with respect to young people. Definitions of the various ages of responsibility, of the workings of the Children and Young Persons Acts, and the making of care and detention orders, all aroused considerable interest. Somewhat surprisingly, because it was presumably no novelty, the visit of an administrative colleague from the local education authority office was looked forward to with keen anticipation, and the meeting proved most lively. Descriptions by visiting speakers of the reformed social services and the reform of local government were also considered to have been well worth while in providing useful information that would not otherwise have been available and in stimulating a large number of questions.

Specific topics under discussion ranged from particular cases of truancy or family breakdown, with the attendant social and economic characteristics of the family, to the way in which the school encouraged parental interest and how parents could legitimately become more involved. Issues of parent education and the optimum time for its provision, and the need for teacher retraining and the provision of funds to enable the schools to develop a more community-centred commitment, were discussed openly and critically. In the inner-city school the opinion emerged strongly that the problem of the large immigrant minority often demanded disproportionate time and attention. There was always a wealth of contributions on how better contact could be established with the immigrant communities and a concern to try to understand their special problems. Contact with parents, particularly by male teachers, was often very difficult in cases where religious and cultural traditions made home-visiting out of the question. Discussion of such issues as truancy and the local authority's policy with regard to the prosecution of parents of persistent truants was a recurring area of controversy. This latter problem emerged as one of considerable importance, for here, probably for the first time, it was possible for the differing views of the education welfare officer, the police and the school to come together in a fruitful discussion. Somewhat to our surprise, it was the teachers who pressed most vigorously for a more authoritarian and clear-cut attitude to truancy, but other issues also highlighted the piecemeal and uncoordinated way in which the effects of deprivation are tackled.

A major issue which arose consistently in all three of the group discussions concerned the way in which the expanding social and pastoral role of the school should be given greater weight when assessing and calculating staff–pupil ratios. In particular, group members raised the fundamental question of whether, for example, teachers, who are expected to give ever more of their time over and above what they have done in the past, should receive extra payment.

But it was clear that such matters needed to be considered as a part of the wider strategy which is being demanded to improve the quality of community life. It was apparent from the teacher groups that there was a need for improved knowledge of and communication with the education welfare, social and legal services, and also better communication internally within the school. The amount of information about children and its availability was a very controversial issue, with some teachers mentioning the danger that teachers could be prejudiced against a child if they had too much information about him. One achievement, perhaps the major (if modest) achievement of the in-service part of the project, was the way in which these public services, all of which support the child in the home and in the school, were brought closer together; and whereas, previously, good relationships had existed mainly between senior officers in the various services, there was now also better communication at grass-roots level. Our feeling at the end of the project was that such communication would continue to need fostering and support. It was clear that the achievement would not be a once-and-for-all job.

One major turning point is worth mentioning. Mid-way through the first term in the inner-city School 2, during the course of a discussion on the inter-relationship of the school with the social services, the previously sceptical headteacher turned to the university tutor and said:

You know we meet together regularly within the staff room and have an op-portunity to discuss this sort of thing. But, if you had not come here and deliberately organized this meeting on Wednesday evenings, then the staff might never have taken such an opportunity of coming together over a cup of tea and talking about the problems of the school and its relationship with its com-munity in this particular way.

This was indeed high praise from one who, at the outset, had been doubtful of the nature of the work we proposed to do and the way in which the project might develop.

At the end of the last session of the academic year, evaluation forms (see Appendix V) were distributed to teachers who had attended any sessions of the teachers' groups. On these, teachers were invited to comment on various aspects of the programme, and, if appropriate, to make suggestions for future work. Owing to the end-of-year rush, returns in one of the three schools were low, but of those who had regularly attended the provision in the other two schools a majority responded, and ninety per cent of those who had responded considered the provision and the experience worthwhile. Clearly, the num-bers involved are too small to be treated other than with great caution. But, despite the small-scale nature of the project, the in-service programme was monitored and evaluated, and at the risk of over-simplifying, the tentative results of the evaluation are given in this chapter.

Teachers were invited to express an opinion about the organization of the course, its content and the assumptions the programme made with regard to the prior knowledge of the teachers. The vast majority of teachers making a return on the in-service work felt that the sessions had been at least satisfactory. About half were of the opinion that they had been well worth while. The content, organization and level also appear to have been favourably regarded, the general ideas and structure apparently having been sufficiently clear, and with an appropriate balance of theoretical and applied work which did not make over-ambitious assumptions about previous knowledge. Interestingly enough, the main criticisms were of the early part of the programme, when there had been less teacher participation in the discussion of the work.

The teachers were further asked to attempt to estimate the effect they felt the in-service programme had had on them. Again, whilst this is a very impressionistic result, the majority felt that the course had had some positive usefulness, while a smaller proportion felt that the sessions had produced a considerable amount of gain for them. Explicit criticisms were few, but, on the other hand, one matter for concern on our part was the extent to which personal work had been generated by the sessions, and a large minority of the teachers who made a return said that they had done no personal reading or research as a result of the course to increase their knowledge of the areas covered. However, an equal number said that they had done selected study with a reading emphasis on some areas of special interest, and a further small group indicated that they had done general study or reading only.

The teachers were also asked whether they felt that the sessions gave them, personally, an opportunity for useful discussion, and provided an opportunity for contrasting views to be heard and discussed. Of those who made returns, the overwhelming majority felt that they had had an opportunity for useful discussion and that the sessions had given an opportunity for contrasting views to be heard and discussed.

Clearly, as we have already emphasized, the results of such a small-scale project must be interpreted with extreme caution. The fact that it was small-scale and school-based contributed in most cases to ongoing good relationships within the school. This very openness, however, caused disappointing results from a statistical point of view, since the project workers wished to enable anyone who had taken part in any of the sessions at any of the three schools to have the opportunity to comment on the work which had taken place, and this made for a low overall response rate to the in-service evaluation forms. But at least some small effort was made within the very limited finance available to this project to achieve some more reliable basis for an assessment of the in-service work, in contrast to the almost total lack of monitoring of other in-service provision made by local education authorities, colleges and universities.

Too many variables are involved in such a situation to permit generalizations of our findings to other areas, but a number of general comments may be made concerning this part of our work. The expectation of resistance, writ so large in the literature of organizational innovation, proved, in the case of two of our schools, to be minimal. It seems certain that this was due to a number of favourable factors, such as the calibre of the staff involved, the healthy tradition of in-service provision in the local education authority, the informal 'tea and biscuits' atmosphere, and not least the co-operation and support and, in one case, enthusiastic and critical interest of the headteacher. The time of day at which the sessions were arranged, their relative brevity, and the fact that they took place in schools, also helped to produce a favourable atmosphere.

Secondly, two points which were highlighted in our own work were the need, on the one hand, for clarity concerning what the innovation involved, and, on the other hand, the provision of expertise to give support to innovatory roles. It is difficult to escape the conclusion that development of the much discussed and little understood community school, pressed on us by the polemic of educationists, is premature until these two conditions of extra support and greater clarity of definition have been met. Our own work seems to suggest that there is a long road to travel before the reality of greater community involvement is achieved, and not a little concern on the part of teachers that the school is increasingly becoming the factotum which can be blamed for all society's ills.

While clearly there is a need for caution in claiming long-term effects, it is possible also to point to quite concrete results that were achieved by the in-service work, not least the way in which it was appreciated by, and satisfying to, both parties. However, perhaps one of the most important achievements was the strengthening of the lines of communication between teachers and the various social, legal and educational services. In this latter connection, the encouragement of an atmosphere where taken-for-granted procedures for pastoral care and the involvement of parents could be discussed critically in a detached and principled manner seemed one of the major attractions of a school-based in-service provision. Similar provision, our experience suggests, could easily be carried out on a modest scale with very limited resources in a larger number of schools.

The crucial importance of deliberate, definitive and systematic provision of in-service courses as part of action-research projects seems to highlight the hollowness of much of the contemporary debate concerning the establishment of community schools, where questions of resources and training have been submerged by 'glossy magazine' considerations of bricks and mortar. Resource considerations of different kinds are all equally important and the last word in this section might appropriately be left to the head of one of the schools. Writing in the project's second working document, *Paper II: An Interim Report*, he expressed the view that:

... if society feels a serious commitment to either community schools or more sophisticated parent–teacher relationships (and the latter is a branch of the former) then sufficient investment will have to be made in *selected* urban areas.

Such questions as the three-session day will have to be seriously discussed with teachers, and members of the community, and any such development organized on a competent and completely professional basis. I do not think that ad hoc arrangements, however 'voluntary' or enthusiastic, can give the conception reality or sustain it once it has life.

10 The parents' views

The parents' questionnaires were distributed to five schools in all, two of which were pilot schools (both these schools were on relatively new housing estates, one being a combined first and middle school, the other a secondary comprehensive). After the distribution and return of the questionnaire from the two pilot schools, slight modifications of the questionnaire were made, in order to include extra and important items such as the birthplace of the father.

The response rates for the five schools ranged from 95·8% to 53·6%, varying from the exceptionally high response rate received from a small, cohesive and highly co-operative pilot school, to a rather poor rate for the largest secondary school, which had an active parent–teacher association and a large proportion of middle-class parents (School 3). Despite the length and complexity of the questionnaire, it nevertheless seemed an appropriate method of collecting sociological data in the types of school with which we worked. It was a matter of some surprise to us that the city-centre School 2, with a high proportion of immigrant parents and of parents of social class III and below (see Table 4), achieved a much higher response than a school with a relatively high proportion of middle-class parents. With improvements in design and technique, there is no reason to doubt that the lower response rates could be considerably boosted.

The questionnaires were distributed through the schools and were accompanied by a covering letter from the headteacher or from the project workers. It was at first thought that, in order to help the 'action' part of the work, the choice of approach to parents should remain with the school. In the event, two schools preferred the letter to come from the university, and in the other three the headteacher preferred to do it himself. In view of the large number of immigrant parents in School 2, a letter in Hindi and Punjabi from the local community relations officer was attached.

The results which are quoted in this report refer to the questionnaires which were returned, and 'missing' categories refer not to unreturned questionnaires, but to questions which were not answered by the respondents.

Table 3 shows that there was little difference between the project schools as

Table 3 Average family size by school

| | Average number of children in family: | | |
	School 1	School 2	School 3
Boys	1·55	2·43	1·61
Girls	1·66	2·12	1·67
Total	3·21	4·55	3·28

regards the average number of children in the families of the respondents, with the exception of inner-city School 2.

In addition, background factors were tested for association, and while at Schools 1 and 3 factors affecting group absences (for example, family size) proved to be only slightly significant, at the inner-city School 2 there was a highly significant relationship between those parents who said they were not satisfied with the school and those whose children had a large number of absences (i.e. over 40 out of 380 possible absences). Moreover, in the same school even the small number of parents who were in lower middle-class occupations had children who were absent from school more often than would have been expected. In all three schools, those parents who were satisfied with the school and had children who liked the school tended to have significantly fewer child absences—and it was these parents who, in turn, were more likely to have visited the school.

The social class of the parents by occupation differed significantly between the three schools, as indicated in Table 4. Clearly School 2 had fewer middle-class parents and more lower working-class parents, and after analysis this

Table 4 Social class by occupation of father (%*)

| | Social class† | | | | | | |
	I	II	IIIN	IIIM	IV	V	Other
School 1	0·5	7	12	43	15	10	13
School 2	0·6	6	3	28	17	20	24
School 3	11	15	13	36	7	3	15

Notes
 * Percentages have been rounded, so that in this, and some subsequent, tables figures do not always add up to exactly 100.
 † I = professional occupations; II = intermediate occupations; IIIN = skilled occupations—non-manual; IIIM = skilled occupations—manual; IV = partly skilled occupations; V = unskilled occupations.

proved to be an important factor, for across all schools there was, as might be expected, a highly significant association between the father's occupation and the age at which the child's parents wished it to leave school, with the higher social classes wishing their children to stay on longer regardless of the school attended.

Similar important differences were found between the schools in terms of place of birth of parents. Again, School 2 was shown to be significantly different from the other schools, with well under half the parents being born in this country, and it was, as expected, the immigrant parents who tended to visit the school less frequently. It must be added, however, that this did not seem to be due to any lack of ambition on the part of the immigrant parents for their children. On the contrary, parents of Asian origin tended to wish their children to stay on at school very much longer than one would have expected, although they tended to be less critical of the school and what it taught. Countries of origin of parents for the three project schools are given in Table 5.

Table 5   Place of birth—fathers and mothers (%)

	Hants.	Rest of England & Wales	Ireland	Continent of Europe	Indian subcontinent	West Indies	Other
School 1:							
Father	87·9	7·0	1·8	1·8	0·4	0·7	0·4
Mother	88·2	5·5	0·4	2·6	0·4	0·7	2·2
School 2:							
Father	43·8	1·7	3·4	4·5	36·0	6·7	3·9
Mother	43·3	6·7	—	3·9	35·4	7·3	3·4
School 3:							
Father	82·8	11·4	2·2	0·6	0·6	0·9	1·5
Mother	84·3	10·5	0·9	0·9	0·6	0·9	1·9

Overall, in terms of the three main indicators of family size, proportion of families in the lower socio-economic groups and proportion of children from immigrant families, School 2 was significantly different from the other schools surveyed. How these factors influenced the parents' attitude to the schools cannot be answered unequivocally on the basis of a small pilot study. However, it seems clear that inner-city schools such as the one included in our survey are suffering from multiple disadvantages which in some cases have a cumulative effect on the extent of home–school relations, which in turn make specific extra-curricular demands on teachers.

The results of analysis of the parents' views on what the schools provided indicated considerable divergences across the three schools. Table 6 refers to the three project schools and is based on information collected from them. Facilities (such as open days, talks on education etc.) are listed in the left-hand column, and 'Yes' or 'No' under the column for each school according to

Table 6　Facilities provided by Schools 1, 2 and 3 (where a facility was available, the % of parents who thought it was *not* provided is shown in brackets)

Facilities	Whether facility provided:					
	School 1		School 2		School 3	
Open evenings	Yes	(0·4)	Yes	(14·6)	Yes	(1·2)
Open days	Yes	(27·2)	No		No	
Talks on education	Yes	(19·9)	Yes	(21·9)	Yes	(8·9)
Opportunities to talk to the headteacher	Yes	(5·1)	Yes	(12·4)	Yes	(13·8)
Opportunities to talk to the child's teacher	Yes	(1·8)	Yes	(8·4)	Yes	(1·8)
A parents' or parent–teacher association (PTA)	No		No		Yes	(0·3)
Opportunities for parents to help at school	Yes	(45·2)	No		Yes	(11·4)
Information on how parents can help the child	Yes	(30·9)	Yes	(28·1)	Yes	(20·9)
Evening classes for parents	Yes	(59·2)	No		Yes	(6·2)
A newsletter/magazine	Yes	(16·2)	Yes	(12·4)	Yes	(11·4)
Information on what and how the child is taught	Yes	(22·8)	Yes	(28·7)	Yes	(26·8)
Out of school activities during school holidays	No		Yes	(19·7)	No	

whether or not the opportunity was provided. Where a facility was available, the percentage of responding parents who none the less thought it was not provided is shown in brackets. Even allowing for methodological flaws, and misunderstanding on the part of parents, it is clear that the schools still had a long way to go in 'selling' the valuable opportunities for closer co-operation which they offered to the parents. Thus, in spite of the fact that all schools, when asked, said that they provided information to parents on what and how children were taught, roughly a quarter of the parents were of the opinion that such information was not provided. Moreover, in each case between eighteen per cent and thirty per cent of the parents who *were* aware that such knowledge was provided were of the opinion that too little information was provided, and a further ten to twenty per cent (approximately) said that they did not know. Indeed, if, in addition to the inaccuracy of the parents' knowledge of what was provided, one takes into account the large proportion of parents who quite clearly did not know about the opportunities offered, there is, in spite of all efforts by the schools involved, a serious communications gap, which should be capable of reduction by systematic testing of different kinds of communication techniques between the school and parents.

All three schools in the project could, with great benefit, provide parents with more information about the schools, although clearly School 3 does seem to have been substantially more successful in this respect than the other two schools. Thus, even in schools which are in an area of the country which is relatively prosperous and has a good standard of educational provision, parents are still inadequately informed about what the school offers, although of course this communications gap does not reflect any lack of interest on the part of schools nor a lack of effort (indeed, our impression from working with the schools is quite the contrary). Clearly, if parents are to be persuaded to become more involved, schools need to develop new strategies, including improved methods of communication in addition to those already tried, in order to inform parents of what they provide.

Parents were also asked if they knew any of the governors at their child's school and whether they thought parents and teachers should be made school governors. The responses, if perhaps not surprising, were disappointing in the context of a society which prides itself on being democratic. As expected the overwhelming majority of parents did not know any school governors at all

Table 7 Number of school governors known by given percentages of parents

Number of governors known by parents	School 1	School 2	School 3
All governors known	0·7	0·6	—
Some known	15·8	13·5	11·1
None known	82·4	85·4	87·4
'Missing'	1·1	0·6	1·5

(see Table 7), but perhaps even more interesting were the attitudes which they held with regard to participation by parents and teachers in the government of schools (see Table 8). Possibly because of fears of interference by other parents in the education of their children, or perhaps because of a lack of

Table 8 Parents' views on parents' and teachers' membership of school governing bodies (%)

Parents' replies		School 1	School 2	School 3
Parents should be members	Agree	36·4	28·7	40·9
	Disagree	60·7	68·0	57·2
	'Missing'	2·9	3·4	1·8
Teachers should be members	Agree	50·4	47·8	53·2
	Disagree	43·7	44·9	43·4
	'Missing'	5·9	7·3	3·4

understanding of what participation might involve, there are substantial reservations on the part of the majority of parents with regard to parents being members of governing bodies, and there is clearly more support amongst parents for teachers adopting this role. This result may be influenced by the fact that the vast majority of responding parents across all project schools seemed satisfied with the schools, and most children seemed, according to their parents, to like school. Even if one interprets this as the opinions of an uncritical clientele—in itself a dangerous assumption—it is clear that innovations involving greater parental participation in school government have a weighty task of parent education to reckon with if they are to be successful. Moreover, even given the continuance of the present system, there is a substantial task of explanation and communication if school governors are not to continue to be considered remote and unknown.

Other innovations may have to reckon with similar difficulties. For example, parents were asked to say whether they were in favour of home-visiting, and although we have no way of knowing to what extent the full implications of this question were understood by parents (and all the *caveats* about asking parents 'new' questions in action-research must apply until such a time as the concept is established), the replies were significant. Parents were asked if, in matters concerning their child, they would like a home-visit. The replies which they gave are indicated in Table 9.

Table 9 Parents' views on whether they would like a home-visit by teachers and others (%)

Parents' replies	Visit by headteacher	Visit by child's teacher	Visit by school counsellor
School 1:			
Parents answering 'yes'	30	43	54
Parents answering 'no'	56	46	36
School 2:			
Parents answering 'yes'	33	46	49
Parents answering 'no'	44	32	29
School 3:			
Parents answering 'yes'	22	45	55
Parents answering 'no'	68	46	37

One of the most striking features of this table is the indication which it gives of the hesitancy of parents, in all three schools, concerning home-visiting. Even given a specialized school counsellor, roughly one third of parents would still not want a home-visit, and it is clear that the majority of parents would not wish for home-visits by the headteacher. We did not seek the reasons for this result, but such reasons, and the wishes of parents in the matter of home-visiting, will need to be taken into account in any future policy concerning extended roles for the teacher. Perhaps the social/educational distance implicit in the role of the teacher makes it inevitable that teachers as a whole may never be welcomed as home-visitors. However, there are contrary indications from the action side of our work, and certainly two of the parent-group leaders reported that their parents' group was firmly of the opinion that they would welcome home-visits by teachers. The groups felt quite strongly that the initial diffidence would be overcome by explanation and understanding; once again the importance of change being explained to those involved in it is underlined by our results. Certainly, this is an aspect of home–school relations to which any further major study would have to give particular attention.

The Schools Council's report *Enquiry 1: Young School Leavers* (HMSO, 1968) attempted an extensive analysis of the attitudes of parents of fifteen-year-old leavers towards various functions of the school and discovered that both the leavers and their parents saw the main functions of the school as being those which would provide knowledge and skills, and which would promote the achievement of vocational success, but that they less frequently regarded the school as having responsibility in the field of development of personality and character. Parents were, however, particularly concerned about the standards of discipline; they also felt that insufficient attention was being paid to writing, arithmetic, spelling and speech.

Our own survey dealt with the parents of children in the final three years of compulsory secondary education, although across a much smaller and statistically less viable sample. Broadly speaking, the above results previously referred to were confirmed by our work. By far the largest number of parents in each of the three schools felt that the teaching of writing, reading and arithmetic was very important, and other vocationally-oriented skills were on the whole highly scored by parents. Non-vocational aims were rated less highly amongst parents in all three schools, and in each school approximately one parent in ten felt that teaching the child to enjoy his/her leisure was unimportant. Broader school objectives were even less highly rated but there was, even so, a fairly large mandate for the school to pursue policies of community and parent education.

Thus, an overview of how parents regarded various aims of formal education was obtained. When the results of these overviews were analysed and related to other factors, such as social class, it was found that parents in the higher socio-economic groups tended to think that provision for community and parent education was unimportant, while parents of working-class families tended to regard it as very important. Significantly fewer working-class parents regarded education for the whole community as unimportant. Although caution is needed in interpreting the data, there was on this issue a highly significant difference between parents and teachers in the inner-city school, with the teachers attaching greater importance to community education. In the same school, which had the largest proportion of immigrant school-children, the questions concerning the aims of education were also tested for significant differences between immigrant and non-immigrant parents (Table 10). It was evident that there was a significant difference

Table 10   Differences between immigrant and non-immigrant parents in the inner-city school with regard to given aims of education

Aims	% of parents who considered given aims very important	
	Immigrant	*Non-immigrant*
Help the child to be happy	50	74
Teach him/her to enjoy leisure	17	36
Provide him/her with out-of-school activities, e.g. clubs	17	43
Prepare the child for being grown-up	35	66

Note
The differences between immigrants and non-immigrants were in all cases statistically significant at the 1% level.

between the way in which immigrant and non-immigrant parents considered it to be the school's responsibility to provide education for leisure, with immigrant parents also attributing less importance to a community role for the school. This may, of course, be due to immigrant parents knowing even less about the idea of a community school than the English parents, but it may also indicate quite strong divergences in the meaning attached to the word 'school' by different races, cultures and social classes.

Parent satisfaction with schools

We have already drawn attention to the high level of satisfaction which parents expressed with all schools surveyed. In addition to the general questions, a Likert Scale of various aspects of school life and activity was constructed and parents were invited to express agreement or disagreement with particular items. When asked whether they were happy with what the school was doing for their child, roughly four out of every five parents indicated that they were and only a small proportion said that they were not, although there were significant differences between different schools. However, in general, over half of the parents who responded agreed or strongly agreed that they were happy with the schools, that the teachers made them feel at home and that the schools were 'go-ahead'. Parents of all three project schools were of the opinion that the teachers were capable of teaching the child without the parents help. Overall, when the replies of those parents who responded 'agree' or 'strongly agree' were put together, the proportion of parents was as indicated in Table 11.

Table 11   Parents who agreed or strongly agreed with certain statements about their child's school (%)

Statements	School 1	School 2	School 3
I am happy with what the school is doing for my child	86·7	82·0	86·5
The school is go-ahead	70·1	61·2	69·0
The teachers make me feel at home when I visit the school	75·6	59·6	75·5
Parents have enough say in *what* their children are taught	28·8	33·7	33·4
Parents have enough say in *how* their children are taught	28·4	30·9	27·0
The teachers are capable of teaching my child without my help	70·1	71·3	69·3
There is enough contact between the parents and the teachers	51·3	42·1	58·6

However, within this overall picture there were important differences which will need to be taken into account in strategies adopted by any future major project. In one school, parents of larger families agreed or strongly agreed that parents have sufficient say in how their children are taught, whilst parents of smaller families disagreed or strongly disagreed. This response reflects the desire on the part of those with smaller families, mostly middle-class, to know more about and have a greater influence on teaching methods in schools. In the inner-city school parents in the higher socio-economic groups tended to feel that they did not have sufficient influence over what their children were taught, and yet these were the very parents who were more inclined to say that the teachers made them feel at home when they visited the school. On the other hand, fewer immigrant parents than expected in the inner-city School 2 felt that the teachers made them feel at home, although they were not espe-cially dissatisfied with the level of contact between parents and teachers, and tended to be significantly less critical of what was taught in that school than non-immigrant parents.

Parents were asked to indicate how frequently they had visited the school (Table 12). There is a wide variation in the number of visits paid to the schools by parents, although there is need for caution in interpreting the results. The

P.T.—3*

question concerning school visits came towards the end of a long question-naire, which must have proved taxing to many parents. This may be one reason for the large number of missing answers, particularly in the inner-city school. Again, memories fade and it is highly likely that many parents genuine-ly could not recollect or had forgotten how many times they had visited the school. Others still may have been afraid that someone was checking up on them, or they may have felt slightly guilty that they had not visited the school more often and thus felt the need to compensate. However, it is apparent that, even given these reservations, substantial numbers of parents in each of the schools had not visited the school at all in the previous year, and that a much

Table 12 Percentage of parents who had visited the school a given number of times

	4 or more times	1–3 times	Not at all	'Missing'
School 1:				
Visits in last year	9·9	73·5	9·2	7·4
Visits since child started at this school	50·4	33·1	6·6	9·9
School 2:				
Visits in last year	11·2	41·6	30·3	16·9
Visits since child started at this school	22·5	34·3	14·0	29·2
School 3:				
Visits in last year	16·2	60·9	19·1	4·0
Visits since child started at this school	56·0	27·7	10·2	6·1

smaller but still substantial number had not visited at all. It is not possible to give an unequivocal answer as to why these parents had not visited; neverthe-less, an analysis was made of the people concerned. It was found, for example, that immigrant parents at School 2 tended to visit the school less frequently than expected, showing a highly significant difference from non-immigrants in this respect. As expected, parents in middle-class occupations and mothers with a more protracted education tended to visit the school more frequently than parents from working-class occupations and those mothers with a less extensive school education.

In the school with the largest proportion of middle-class parents (School 3), parents did not seem to be visiting the school as frequently as might, in view of the social-class composition of the school, have been expected, which was somewhat puzzling in view of the well-organized parent–teacher association.

One explanation may be that parents did not consider visits to PTA meetings as being visits to the school, another that the desire for school-visiting was channelled by the PTA's very existence.

There was a significant difference between the frequency of visiting at School 2 and at the other two schools, a difference which highlighted the problems which the inner-city school encounters in fostering parental visiting to the school. Moreover, when all schools were taken together and the proportions of parents who had not visited the school since their child began were associated with the social class of the father, it became apparent that, as a generalization, parents in the lower socio-economic groups tended to visit less frequently, if at all. Linked with this was the highly significant relationship, mentioned previously, between the father's occupation and the age the child was expected to leave school, for all schools taken as one group, The higher social classes thus signalled their interest in their child's education by visiting the school more frequently and being more overtly ambitious for him.

In conclusion, the opportunity afforded the parents to comment in anonymity on their schools seems to have been well received and responsibly used. With significant exceptions most parents at all the schools seemed to be relatively satisfied with what the schools were doing for their children and in each case there appears to have been a pool of latent goodwill towards the school and the teachers. On the other hand there are, quite naturally, areas where greater co-operation, information and opportunity would appear to be desirable if the 'educational covenant'* between parents, teachers and other lay and professional groups in the community is to be made more flexible and yet more effective.

The kind of information which we collected for the project schools, and which we fed back to the schools within two months of the distribution of the questionnaire, should be available at intervals to all secondary schools as an aid to their policy-making in this area. It is within the scope of all schools— for example, teachers studying for further qualifications could well undertake such a task—and it is crucial if the reality as well as the ideal of greater community involvement in formal education is to be achieved.

---

* This term is used by the Schools Council Working Party on the Whole Curriculum in its report, *The Whole Curriculum 13–16*, Schools Council Working Paper 54 (Evans/Methuen Educational, 1975). (See especially Chapter III.)

11 The teachers' views

In this chapter we seek to discuss some of the views expressed by teachers during the project, and which were collected either in the form of bespoke data from questionnaires or in individual comment or group discussion. In doing this, we make no pretence of being able to regard these opinions as having universal validity for all secondary schools, let alone for the teaching profession as a whole. Whatever social facts are reproduced here are given as a basis for discussion amongst parents and amongst teachers, and between members of the two groups. It is intended that the facts should provide a challenge, something for people to react to, to ask questions about, to see how far the pattern is the same in their region, area or school—should provide, in fact, some useful starting points as a basis for a more sophisticated and widespread survey. Ultimately, and often in spite of social surveys and research, people will tend to believe what they want to believe and only patient and sensitive persuasion based on the available evidence can change this.

The teacher questionnaire was distributed to all members of staff in the three schools concerned, towards the end of the summer term. This particular time was chosen in order that the collection of data should not conflict with the 'action' part of the work. However, being at the end of a year of action-research, the distribution came at a time when resources, both human and financial, were almost exhausted and the strain of being involved in the year's activities on a part-time basis, in addition to already heavy workloads, was beginning to tell. In addition, the distribution of the questionnaire coincided with the 'coasting' time towards the end of the summer term. Consequently the response rate was disappointingly low. Thus caution is needed in the interpretation of results, and comparisons and analyses given in this chapter are, as we have said, intended more to raise issues than give definitive assessments.

We have referred previously to the substantial staffing differences in the three schools with regard to age, status and qualification (see Table 2). The fact that almost three quarters of the teachers in School 2 were over forty years of age, and that only one was in the age bracket twenty to twenty-four, is indicative of wider problems faced by the school in achieving a staffing balance.

It might be, for example, that the physical conditions of the school were such as to deter the recruitment of younger staff who might have effectively added a further dimension in assisting the school to fight its multiple disadvantages. Again, although highly qualified specialists are by no means always the best teachers, the fact that School 2 also had the smallest number of staff with degree-level qualifications or diplomas in education is significant in connection with the kinds of difficulties which it faced.

There was an almost equal distribution of men and women amongst the respondents and roughly three quarters of the teachers in our sample were married, the majority having children of their own.

Broadly speaking, teachers in all schools tended to be satisfied with the present level of contact between home and school, and more specifically with the opportunities given to parents to be involved in the life of the school. In addition, those who were married and had children of their own tended, in their capacity as parents, to be satisfied with the opportunities given to parents to help at school, and considered the provision of social functions for parents to be adequate. What differences did emerge were marginal, and it is possible to give the teachers' view as a whole with regard to specific functions. Table 13 gives a review of the opinions of the teachers in our sample on given facets of home–school relations. On the whole, there was a high level of satisfaction with the state of home–school relations, with the main area for improvement being seen as the provision of formal opportunities for the parents to hear more about education.

There seem to be few surprises in the teachers' responses, which in general seemed to reflect a sober mixture of caution and realism. One might expect that teachers who are already hard pressed in their workload and consider that they are underpaid would feel that they and their school were sufficiently involved with parents, and certainly this was an opinion which seemed to be confirmed by the teacher discussion groups, where there was a marked feeling that such developments as the community school (which would involve greater community commitment by teachers) should be put on a fully professional basis. In some cases, this apparently indicated an increasing awareness of the 'role-overload' which teachers were experiencing and the need for them to have specialist assistance. Home-visiting was a case in point, where the overwhelming majority of teachers were in favour of a school counsellor for this function; a large minority tended to have misgivings about teachers being required to make visits, with the majority being against home-visiting by headteachers. Table 14 gives our indication of the views of teachers responding to this question.

The concept of the community school is well on the way to becoming one of the major educational bandwagons of our age. But the response which we received from teachers, when the question of greater community involvement in education was raised, was Delphic to say the least. The abstention rate was

Table 13 Teachers' opinions about existing provision for parents (% of teachers)

Facilities for parents	Too much provided	Enough provided	Too little provided	Not provided	Don't know	'Missing'
Open evenings	—	87·5	5·4	3·6	1·8	1·8
Open days	—	42·9	5·4	39·3	3·6	8·9
Talks for parents on education	—	42·9	23·2	14·3	14·3	5·4
Opportunities for parents to talk to the headteacher	—	72·3	5·4	3·6	16·1	1·8
Opportunities for parents to talk to the teacher	—	83·9	10·7	1·8	1·8	1·8
A parent–teacher association (PTA)	3·6	42·9	1·8	39·3	7·1	5·4
Opportunities for parents to help at the school	—	39·3	23·2	26·8	8·9	1·8
Information on how parents can help their child	—	42·9	26·8	8·9	16·1	5·4
A newsletter/ magazine	—	67·9	12·5	10·7	7·1	1·8
Information for parents on what and how their child is taught	—	55·4	23·2	14·3	5·4	1·8
Out-of-school activities during holidays	—	64·3	10·7	12·5	10·7	1·8

Table 14 Teachers' attitudes to home-visiting (%)

Home-visiting	Yes	No	Don't know	'Missing'
By the headteacher	17·9	63·3	14·3	3·6
By the child's teacher	50·0	37·5	12·5	—
By the school counsellor	85·7	7·1	7·1	—

high, and although roughly two fifths of the teachers felt that their school should develop into a community school, a similar proportion had heard nothing about such institutions. A similar uncertainty was apparent on the question of the school providing education for the whole community, including adults (see Table 15). Clearly, parent education was not estimated as being as important for the school as its more conventional objectives and functions; none the less, three quarters of teachers felt that the school had an intermediary role in helping parents to understand their children.

The role of the teacher as surrogate counsellor is not something which is alien to British education; indeed, it could be argued that this was a substantial part of the role of a teacher in former times, in smaller schools, and in rural and small urban communities. Whether such a function can in modern circumstances be more than a romantic hangover is open to dispute, but it would certainly involve teachers in the learning of new skills at initial and in-service levels; well over half of the teachers recognized this, although many remained unconvinced. Roughly three quarters of teachers felt that a strengthening of links between the school and the community would involve a changing of attitudes on the part of teachers; at the same time they were convinced that courses could be supplied to assist in the necessary changes. However, only a very small minority felt that such courses were being provided for them at the moment. If the teaching profession and society really want to pursue such objectives as the community school implies, the implications for in-service education are obvious. The teachers' views were clear: if society wants the community school, it must pay and train for it.

Time and again it seemed to us that, in our discussion with parents and teachers and in the returns to our questionnaires, the issue of an expanded community commitment to the existing adult education system was being raised. Whilst the concepts of lifelong and continuing education throughout life have taken their place in the polemic of educational politicians, the relationship that these concepts might imply between the adult educational and formal educational systems remains hazy and uncertain. The ideas of Paulo Freire* (the Brazilian adult educator) and Mao Tse Tung have been challenging the unwarranted bookishness of much contemporary education, and it could be that a clear association of adult education provision with the secondary system of education, on an end-on basis but on the terms of the secondary system, would be the kiss of death to a more dynamic and socially relevant adult education. It could be that it is the existing adult education agencies which are the only ones capable of marshalling and organizing the resources necessary for an appropriate inter-professional training for teachers.

Teachers' views on the aims of the school were by no means formal and scholastic. There was considerable support amongst teachers for education for leisure, and for the development of the whole child; indeed, as previous

* Paulo Freire, *Pedagogy of the Oppressed*, trans. M. B. Ramos (Sheed & Ward, 1972).

Table 15 Teachers' views on the aims of schools (%)

Aims of school	Very important	Important	Don't know	Unimportant	'Missing'
Teach the child reading/writing/arithmetic	91·1	7·1	—	1·8	—
Help him/her to pass exams and to get a good job later	25·0	69·6	—	1·8	3·6
Help the child to be happy	67·9	28·6	—	—	3·6
Teach the child the difference between right and wrong	80·4	17·9	—	—	1·8
Teach him/her discipline	69·6	25·0	3·6	1·8	—
Help the child to develop fully all his/her abilities	89·3	10·7	—	—	—
Develop respect for law and order	64·3	26·8	3·6	3·6	1·8
Develop his/her imagination	66·1	32·1	—	—	1·8
Teach him/her to enjoy leisure	60·7	35·7	3·6	—	—
Provide him/her with out-of-school activities, e.g. clubs	23·2	62·5	5·4	5·4	3·6
Prepare the child for being grown-up	57·1	35·7	3·6	3·6	—
Help parents to understand their children	23·2	50·0	14·3	8·9	3·6
Provide education for all the community including adults	26·8	39·3	12·5	21·4	—
Teach the child not to accept authority uncritically	25·0	37·5	17·9	17·9	1·8

research* has indicated, when teacher and parent responses were compared, parents tended to emphasize more heavily than teachers the traditional vocational role of the school in helping children to pass examinations and get a good job later. As a basis for discussion, Table 15 gives a review of teachers' responses to questions relating to some of the aims of the school.

We were interested not only in teachers' views of the school, but also how teachers thought the parents viewed the school. Roughly three quarters of the teachers indicated that, in their opinion, most parents were happy with what the school was doing for their children, and approximately the same proportion expressed the view that the parents felt at home when they visited the school. But on the question of whether parents were happy with what the schools were doing for their children there were significant differences of opinion between parents and teachers in all three schools, with the parents feeling less happy than the teachers supposed.

Roughly two out of every five teachers thought that there was insufficient contact between parents and teachers, whereas a slightly smaller proportion thought the opposite. Linked with this result was the somewhat alarming opinion of roughly three out of every four teachers that they were capable of teaching the child without the parents' help, and the fact that the majority of teachers thought that parents had enough say in what and how their children were taught. There seems little prospect of an immediate welcome amongst teachers for greater parental say in determining the content of the curriculum and methods of teaching, and further investigation is clearly desirable as regards how, within the context of a democratic society, such a development might take place. We raise this issue again in our concluding chapter. To some extent we allow the views of teachers on their schools to speak for themselves, and these are given in Table 16.

There were highly significant divergences of opinion amongst teachers and parents on the extent to which it was felt that parents had sufficient say in the school, and these divergences were not related to parental satisfaction or dissatisfaction with the school. From this and the broader evidence of development elsewhere it seems safe to say that the former cosy consensus between parents and teachers is gradually changing. The implications of such a development are clear in terms of a painful (if necessary) re-negotiation of the contractual relationship between parents and the professional, political, lay and administrative people at present in control of our schools. If the current tactical discussion of participation is eventually to lead to the community school, there is a need for the redefinition of strategic objectives, which will clearly involve a redefinition of the concept 'school' not just for parents but for teachers too. The stereotype of the domineering middle-class parent is often used as the fall-guy by the illiberal, who want no greater participation of parents than can be easily handled. But the answer to this is that a wider

* *Enquiry 1:Young School Leavers* (HMSO, 1968).

Table 16 Teachers' views on their schools (%)

Statements put to teachers	Strongly agree	Agree	Don't know	Disagree	Strongly disagree	'Missing'
Most parents are happy with what the school is doing for their children	12·5	64·3	12·5	5·4	—	5·4
The school is go-ahead	12·5	48·2	16·1	17·9	—	5·4
We make the parents feel at home when they visit the school	30·4	46·4	16·1	—	1·8	5·4
Parents have enough say in *what* their children are taught	14·3	41·1	12·5	25·0	1·8	5·4
Parents have enough say in *how* their children are taught	17·9	44·6	12·5	16·1	3·6	5·4
We are capable of teaching the child without the parents' help	10·7	16·1	3·6	57·1	8·9	3·6
There is enough contact between the parents and the teachers	7·1	33·9	8·9	39·3	7·1	3·6

social-class participation will only come about if it is educated for, and this will require a more dynamic adult education movement which has reconsidered its traditional relationship to the social class structure. The community school is no more than an ideal at the moment, which on the basis of our experience neither the majority of teachers nor the majority of parents understands. One wonders whether the educational clairvoyants do either! In a society which is committed, however haltingly, to closer relations between parents and teachers, our findings show limited goodwill on the part of parents and a dispassionate realism on the part of teachers, combined nevertheless with an appreciation, by both groups, of the need for change. The present-day systems of teacher and adult education, often dismissed as being out of touch with the needs of modern communities, will together have to shoulder the burden of community development education; in this operation, parent and teacher discussion groups can, we believe, play a major part. Despite the fact that teacher education and adult education have evolved from very different backgrounds, the development of the concept of the community school demands that they work more closely together in the future.

12 Conclusions and recommendations

Before restating our findings in the form of tentative conclusions it must once again be stressed that this was only a very limited pilot study. We have, with the minimum of financial and human resources, been grappling with proposals concerning relations between the home and the school which are surrounded by the most complex network of established relationships and expectations. Where academic angels might fear to tread, we were forced by circumstances to proceed apace. Our conclusions, therefore, which we hope are supported by the descriptions of the 'action' part of our study and the statistical evidence, are of a pilot nature pointing the way for more extensive and adequately financed research in depth.

Despite our reservations about the validity of conclusions derived from a pilot project we can, with some confidence, commend the value of action-research as an investigatory tool in the field of home–school relations. Traditional methods of observational research might have precluded the setting-up of parent and teacher discussion-groups where attitudes to proposals for improving home–school relations (often of a radical nature) could be recorded and tested. But because action-research blurs the distinction between academic investigation and policy-making it needs to be preceded by painstaking consultation with all concerned, aimed at carefully explaining the objectives of the research. This consultation is an indispensable prerequisite of any successful action-research but in no area is this more acutely felt than in home–school relations. Such consultation should in our opinion result in a consensus of approval for the research objectives which will ensure an invaluable moral commitment on the part of all participating groups to seeing the research through to a successful conclusion.

Once a school has been selected for a programme of effort to improve home–school relations, our experience strongly suggests that the first objective must be a careful study of the social characteristics of the school's catchment area, including details of the socio-economic structure of the community. Family characteristics such as the father's occupation, family size, age and sex of children, and the age parents left school, will provide the school with vital information essential for any planned programme to improve home–school relations. A sensitive approach will be necessary when gathering together information on family backgrounds, but our experience with the parent questionnaire suggests that the majority of parents will readily volunteer these family details if it is first carefully explained that the information will only be used to help improve their child's education. Other characteristics concerning the history of the school, average age of teachers and their formal qualifications, the school curriculum and teaching methods, and the attitude of the head and his staff to pastoral care and links with parents, provide an essential background from which successful teacher and parent discussion-groups can be established.

Our findings confirm that most experienced teachers realize the vital role played by the home in successful child-education, but that they sometimes fail to recognize the highly influential role they themselves can play in determining the attitude of parents to the education of their children. In-service courses for teachers can, in our experience, reinforce their awareness of the social dimensions of education and the pastoral role of the secondary school teacher. The provision of school-based in-service courses has been highlighted by our project as being one means of supplying, on a low cost basis, the skills and expertise so essential in the changing role of the teacher. There is a place for courses in institutions and centres away from the school, but what this project sought to pioneer was a *school-based* provision which could come to grips with the real problems and real cases. What we did is a viable financial proposition for any area, given partnership between the local education authorities, colleges and universities. For such in-service courses to be successful it is necessary for the head of the school concerned to show approval and enthusiasm, and for the staff to be closely involved in the design. This in turn is made infinitely easier if the chief education officer and his staff likewise value the provision of pastoral-care courses. Teacher discussion-groups can also be used to bring busy teachers into closer contact with education welfare officers, youth and community workers, home visitors and other trained social workers who work with schools, but who too often have little contact with teachers.

One most important teacher-attitude to home–school relations emerged from all our discussions with teachers; if more time and effort is required from teachers in order to improve teacher–parent relationships and understanding, either more teachers will be required or extra payment will have to be made. Most of the teachers and heads expressed the view that society and parents were expecting them to play a greater social role, as distinct from a purely educational one, without recognizing this increased responsibility in terms of more teachers, more pay, or both. Clearly, such a question goes far beyond the scope of this report. However, it should be noted that a possible alternative exists, namely the involvement in home–school relations of specialists such as EWOs and school counsellors who, with the assistance of adult educators, could begin to harness the voluntary potential which undoubtedly exists amongst parents. The harnessing of latent voluntary energy and ability by a hard core of trained, experienced and dedicated professionals is, we believe, a possible alternative to the very expensive expansion of teacher numbers and payment. The extent of this possibility can only be determined by more intensive research, which would seek to create such a team of professionals and build up a volunteer force of parents. Existing experience of community development projects suggests that such an approach is viable.

Parent discussion groups, according to our research, provide a most valuable vehicle for the transmission of information about what any particular school is trying to achieve with children. It is possible to recruit the non-participating parent who rarely visits the school, if the discussion group leader or other volunteer makes personal contact, for example by knocking on doors. A parent discussion group with more than about twenty-five members cannot operate through small-group discussion methods, and it may be necessary either to run several meetings at the same time, or to plan a sequence which could cover an average school within a short period. Such a programme of parent education would require a small and expensive army of professional educators and administrators, unless advantage is taken of the latent energy and ability of parents, especially in the recruitment and mobilization of their fellow-parents.

Our work indicates that a majority of parents, while instinctively understanding the importance of the home in the child's education, believe that its influence is minimal compared with that of the processes of formal education. Few parents in our discussion groups believed that the attitude of parents to schools and teachers played the decisive role in their child's education suggested by much research. Any programme of parent education will have to place considerable emphasis upon the social aspects of education.

The parents in our discussion groups expressed considerable interest in modern teaching methods and curricula. Time and again they expressed the view that, compared with their own school experience, modern methods appeared to be much more imaginative and stimulating. Whether, given the pace of change, time will eventually eliminate this 'experience gap' is highly debatable, but in the meantime explanation of what goes on in present-day schools should provide an attractive agenda for parent meetings in particular, and also for other activities such as the 'education shop'. Indeed, given greater co-ordination, there is no reason why each area of a city should not have at least one 'education shop' each year to spread information and enable parents to ask questions.

All this implies that the different bodies responsible for adult education will have to join forces and show much greater concern for parent education than hitherto. We believe that such recommendations are very much in the spirit of the recent Russell Report, *Adult Education: A Plan for Development* (HMSO, 1973).

Our research experience also suggests that parent discussion-groups are probably the only really satisfactory way of introducing to parents some of the more controversial proposals to improve home–school relations, such as parent attendance in classes, home visiting by a member of the school staff, and eventually the community school. Questionnaire and interview methods of obtaining parent opinion are of little use, as they persuade parents to express an opinion on something about which they know almost nothing. You cannot, for example, expect a considered reply to the proposition that home visiting is necessary if what is involved is not first explained. We found in our discussion groups that the views of parents on a new proposition for improving home–school relations changed considerably after the proposition had been carefully explained.

Large secondary schools where there is a specially trained member of staff (such as a school counsellor) with a full-time responsibility for improving home–school relations could, we feel, with the assistance of a willing head, an outside adult-education agency and in-service teacher-training provision, establish teacher and parent discussion groups which could make a long-term impact on parent–teacher relations. If such a *team* approach were adopted, along with the mobilization of voluntary parent assistance, a relatively inexpensive way of improving education, and particularly of supporting children socially and emotionally, could be developed. Further intensive research is necessary, however, to test the feasibility of such a team approach.

Much initial and in-service teacher training places insufficient emphasis upon the importance of the social dimensions of education, and in particular upon the attitude of parents to schools and teachers. Until comparatively recent times, the overwhelming emphasis has been upon subject-training and academic standards. Our research experience with the teacher discussion-groups strongly suggests that experienced teachers attach great importance to the influence of the child's home, parents and peer-group. But because of the weight of tradition and practice, and the low priority given in the promotion stakes to home-school knowledge and expertise, teachers are not encouraged to study and improve home–school relations. If greater importance could be attached to such relations by colleges of education, local education authorities and the providers of in-service training, along with more stress on knowledge and ability in this field when promoting teachers, a great deal could be achieved, we believe, not only in improving child education but also in reducing the growing tensions and problems of discipline within secondary schools.

While care must be taken to preserve educational standards—indeed we would argue that greater parental support would improve them—a great deal can be done to integrate the school more firmly with the local community through a deep involvement of the curriculum with the environment in which the children have grown up and developed. Such an approach need not reduce standards or be inward-looking and unimaginative. And what is lost in terms of a more traditional approach to the school curriculum is gained by reducing the tensions created in the many young children who experience a sharp cultural distinction between school and environment. A school curriculum which reflects the local environment might also help to reduce the distance between parent and teacher. However, we must acknowledge that our research indicates that many parents fear that too much emphasis upon a community-based curriculum could prove a handicap to their children in the examination race.

Just as our work conveys the need for caution concerning a community-based curriculum, it also suggests that the concept of the community school is rarely, if ever, clearly understood by either teachers or parents. Indeed, we have sometimes wondered whether any consensus about the community school exists amongst those professional educationists who so enthusiastically support its development. Before bewildering parents with this somewhat ill-defined (if socially imaginative) proposal, a great deal more solid groundwork needs to be laid down in the form of helping parents to become involved with their child's school at what may appear to be more prosaic levels.

The community school, then, is something we should only proceed towards with caution. Our research also indicates that the majority of parents have little desire to interfere with the way schools are at present organized and controlled. There is scant evidence in our research to indicate that 'parent power' in the management and government of schools is desired by more than a tiny minority of parents. But, on the other hand, there is firm evidence to suggest that many parents would welcome greater information, consultation and involvement in their child's education than is available to them at the moment.

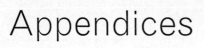

Appendices

Appendix I
Action and research:
the methods of the project

Both the Educational Priority Area projects and the current community development projects used the strategy of action-research. The Halsey Report* devoted a chapter to the concept and implications of action-research; it identified five different approaches and recommended that they could be more widely used in the study of problems of social policy. In this appendix we take up the theme of action-research, seen as one method of improving home–school relations, and we describe the way in which the decision to use this method influenced both the 'action' and 'research' parts of our project.

Action-research is by definition an interventionist approach to policy-making, which challenges the value judgements contained in much contemporary social research. As such, it is most clearly distinguishable from traditional social research in its implicit critique of 'objectivity' and the 'value-free' assumptions which are claimed. Action-research starts from more or less clearly defined policy objectives and attempts to articulate these in terms of a programme of action and research which will lead to more refined policy recommendations and more rapid implementation. Some writers have proposed that the use of the term 'action-research' should be restricted to projects which are relatively small-scale and operating in 'real world' situations. Others have pointed to the need to regard action-research as complementary to rather than replacing traditional research procedures.

The growth in popularity of action-research can be traced to a number of factors. To some extent it is an approach which does no more than attempt to redress the traditional imbalance in western thought between action and reflection. Conventionally, those activities and studies which are 'pure', as opposed to 'applied', have been considered as being of greater value than those which are to do with the practicalities of life. This train of thought is ancient in origin and has been particularly influential in western education. It was accentuated in the period after the Second World War, when the development of computers greatly improved and facilitated statistical analysis, leading to an emphasis that has seemed to be more on testing scientific

* A. H. Halsey (ed.), *Educational Priority*, vol. I: *E.P.A. Problems and Policies* (HMSO, 1972).

theories than on the equally important task of generating new ones. However, the growing importance of action-research may well have a more pragmatic foundation arising from social planning developments in the United States in the 1960s, for it is clear that in major policy developments the amount of data to be collected and the number of parties to be consulted are both of such proportions that the policy decision is often out of date by the time it is made. The time-lag is so great, the loss of initiative so serious, that conventional research approaches to social-policy implementation are proving increasingly inadequate. It is apparent that there is an inherent conflict, though not an insoluble one, between the demands of action and those of research, which may only to some extent be mitigated by dividing the responsibility for these two areas between the personnel of a project (our own project was not of this kind but was 'uni-dimensional', allowing action and research to be combined). Moreover, there has been increasing dissatisfaction, particularly in education, at the apparent sterility of much academic research.

If recent developments in sociological theory have any contribution to make to social policy, it is that they have alerted students of society to the 'internal logic' of social situations, where all participants attribute subjective meanings to their own actions.* This is particularly important when dealing with such complex social relationships as those between parents and teachers. Thus, standing well back from the functioning of a social system such as a school would provide the necessary degree of 'objectivity', but at the same time would prevent the researcher becoming involved to the extent which would be necessary to understand the internal logic of the social life as seen by the participants. A further factor encouraging the development of action-research is the increasing tendency to involve individuals and communities in a 'dialogical' approach to policy-making. The great rallying cry of our age is participation, and the educational system is clearly not untouched by this.

Human social actions are quite obviously the result of certain pressures for social decision which are based on social values. Thus, although it is important for an action-research project such as our own to make explicit from the beginning both its terms of reference and its aims, it is equally crucial for such work to make explicit the value-assumptions upon which it rests. The development of a project where the workers do not aspire to total scientific objectivity but, on the contrary—in order to ensure that the research and action both make a maximum contribution to a clearly defined social policy— are prepared to make concessions to the usual criteria of scientific objectivity and rigour, must inevitably be academically controversial. But social phenomena cannot be regarded as a scientific laboratory where conditions can be

---

* One book which has been particularly influential in this respect is M. F. D. Young (ed.), *Knowledge and Control: New Directions for the Sociology of Education* (Collier-Macmillan, 1971). See also P. Filmer *et al.*, *New Directions in Sociological Theory* (Collier-Macmillan, 1972.)

observed and manipulated *in vacuo* by research workers looking in from outside, and of course this applies to an institution like a school as much as any other. By cutting down the usual time-lag between research and action, and making the two approaches work side-by-side, action-research may in fact represent a more realistic model for planned social action in rapidly changing societies and communities; so far, alas, this has been apparent only at the 'micro' level. However, it must also be added that the approach is still at an early stage of development.

Many action-research projects, particularly in America, have received an unfavourable press, partly because of the so-called 'unscientific' approach of the research components. The academic community has frequently felt unable to endorse the concessions in research methodology which have been made in order to advance the 'action' part of the work, and has found its own suppositions about the comparatively objective basis of much conventional research challenged. The relative sterility of much traditional academic research in the field of education is often overlooked.

The area of relationships between the school and the community, and more precisely between parents and teachers, is one which is fraught with difficulty. There is a wide literature which accepts the importance of improved home–school relationships. But there is little indisputable basis of knowledge on which policy can be formulated, and it would be pretentious for a small pilot project, such as our own, to claim that it had achieved such a basis. Our project sought to intervene in the ordinary functioning of these relationships and to attempt to bring about improvement. But can parent–teacher relations be changed without altering the structure of schools and the pattern of control and authority? It is clear that statutory obligations on the part of schools and education authorities to involve parents within the functioning of the educational system in England and Wales are, where they exist at all, very much weaker than those which have been found necessary in other countries such as the United States, France or West Germany. In the last-named country, parents (and pupils) may participate in the election of headteachers, whose appointment is then subject to re-election after a given number of years. We need to know more of what other educational systems are doing in this direction.

One final point should be made, and this is that the relatively well-documented hostility between teachers and researchers was, in this project, allayed to some extent by the close involvement of the research workers in the schools. This was assisted by the school-based provision of in-service work, organized through discussion and teamwork by the project members and the staffs of the schools. However, it is evident that, even given such close personal involvement, the residue of mistrust and resentment about the development of educational research within schools is sufficient for it to be necessary to alert future projects to the desirability of a long preparatory period: there needs to be an initial phase to enable close relationships to be established, before any attempt is made to begin the research work proper. The major danger in such a phase is, as we see it, that it could under certain cirumstances lead to a conservation of already-existing values and structures. Yet, in spite of this, it is probably the best way of getting lasting and agreed change.

There is always the danger of allowing pressure by important social and, particularly, professional groups to skew the aims of any action-research project, and this danger is likely to be minimized only if relationships of trust are given time to develop. To some extent, too, the outcome is dependent on the project director's ability to steer. Yet it is in the interest of all sections of the community that a more open and accountable approach to the provision of formal education should be developed, lest the educational system itself fall victim to the impractical demands of the de-schoolers. We believe that action-research pursuing well-defined policy objectives can help to achieve many of the changes which schools must face if the hitherto high public esteem of state education is to be maintained.

Appendix II
Questionnaire: survey of parents' views on education

Schools Council project 'Parents and Teachers: A Pilot Survey' (based at University of Southampton)

The results of this form will be used to attempt to improve education. They are completely confidential and it is impossible to trace forms or information to individual parents. Do not write names or addresses on this form. Where possible this form should be completed by both parents/guardians together.

A.1 How many children have you? Number of: Boys ☐
     Girls ☐

A.2 How old is the child who brought this form to you?   Age ☐

A.3 Is the child a boy or a girl? Please tick.   Boy ☐
     Girl ☐

PLEASE NOTE: ALL FOLLOWING QUESTIONS REFER ONLY TO THE CHILD WHO BROUGHT THIS FORM TO YOU

Schools work in different ways without necessarily being better or worse than other schools. Here is a list of arrangements that some schools make. You will find that your school provides some and not others. Please read each item carefully and then tick the box which is *right for you*.

Does your child's school provide any of the following?	*Too much provided*	*Enough provided*	*Too little provided*	*Not provided*	*Don't know*
B.1 Open evenings	☐	☐	☐	☐	☐
B.2 Open days	☐	☐	☐	☐	☐
B.3 Talks on education	☐	☐	☐	☐	☐
B.4 Opportunities to talk to the headteacher	☐	☐	☐	☐	☐

Does your child's school provide any of the following?	Too much provided	Enough provided	Too little provided	Not provided	Don't know
B.5 Opportunities to talk to your child's teacher	☐	☐	☐	☐	☐
B.6 A parents' or parent–teacher association (PTA)	☐	☐	☐	☐	☐
B.7 Opportunities for parents to help at school	☐	☐	☐	☐	☐
B.8 Information on how you can help your child	☐	☐	☐	☐	☐
B.9 Opportunities for parents to help on school outings	☐	☐	☐	☐	☐
B.10 Other social functions for parents e.g. dances	☐	☐	☐	☐	☐
B.11 Hints on what books to get your child and from where	☐	☐	☐	☐	☐
B.12 Evening classes for parents	☐	☐	☐	☐	☐
B.13 A newsletter/magazine	☐	☐	☐	☐	☐
B.14 Books for children to read at home	☐	☐	☐	☐	☐
B.15 Information on what and how your child is taught	☐	☐	☐	☐	☐
B.16 Opportunities for parents to attend school assemblies	☐	☐	☐	☐	☐
B.17 Out-of-school activities during school holidays	☐	☐	☐	☐	☐
B.18 Information about the above activities	☐	☐	☐	☐	☐

PLEASE PUT YOUR TICKS IN THE BOXES WHICH ARE RIGHT FOR YOU

C.1 Generally speaking are you satisfied with the school that your child attends?
Very satisfied ☐
Satisfied ☐
Not satisfied ☐

C.2 Does he/she like school?
Usually ☐
Sometimes ☐
Rarely ☐

Every school has a board of managers or governors. Your child's school has one.

C.3 Do you know any of the school managers or governors?
All ☐
Some ☐
None ☐

C.4 Would you like to know who are the school managers or governors?
Yes ☐
No ☐

C.5 Should parents be made managers or governors?
Yes ☐
No ☐

C.6 Do you read to your child at home?
Frequently ☐
Sometimes ☐
Almost never ☐

C.7 Do you think your child should have school work to do at home?
Yes ☐
No ☐
Don't know ☐

C.8 Does your child belong to the local public library?
Yes ☐
No ☐

C.9 On matters concerning your child would you like a visit in your home from:

(*a*) the headteacher
Yes ☐
No ☐
Don't know ☐

(*b*) your child's teacher
Yes ☐
No ☐
Don't know ☐

(*c*) school counsellor (a teacher specially trained to help a child in difficulties)
Yes ☐
No ☐
Don't know ☐

P.T.—4

Please enter your answer here:

C.10 What else would you like to know about the school?

....

C.11 Is there anything taught in school which you think *should not* be taught?

....

C.12 Is there anything not taught in school which you think *should* be taught?

....

C.13 What is it that you *like* most about your child's school?

....

C.14 What is it that you *dislike* most about your child's school?

....

C.15 What have you heard about community schools?

....

If nothing, please tick here: ☐

We would like you to say how important you feel the following are for the school to try and do. In each case we should like you to tick the box you feel is *right for you.*

		Very important	Important	Don't know	Unimportant
D.1	Teach my child reading/writing/arithmetic	☐	☐	☐	☐
D.2	Help him/her to pass exams and to get a good job later	☐	☐	☐	☐
D.3	Help the child to be happy	☐	☐	☐	☐
D.4	Teach the child the difference between right and wrong	☐	☐	☐	☐
D.5	Teach him/her discipline	☐	☐	☐	☐
D.6	Help the child to develop fully all his/her abilities	☐	☐	☐	☐
D.7	Develop respect for law and order	☐	☐	☐	☐
D.8	Develop his/her imagination	☐	☐	☐	☐

		Very important	Important	Don't know	Unimportant
D.9	Teach him/her to enjoy leisure	☐	☐	☐	☐
D.10	Provide him/her with out-of-school activities, e.g. clubs	☐	☐	☐	☐
D.11	Prepare the child for being grown-up	☐	☐	☐	☐
D.12	Help parents to understand their children	☐	☐	☐	☐
D.13	Provide education for all the community	☐	☐	☐	☐
D.14	Teach the child to question authority	☐	☐	☐	☐

Different parents have different opinions about schools. We should like you to read the following statements and then tick the ones which you feel apply to your child's school.

		Strongly agree	Agree	Don't know	Disagree	Strongly disagree
E.1	I am happy with what the school is doing for my child	☐	☐	☐	☐	☐
E.2	The school is go-ahead	☐	☐	☐	☐	☐
E.3	The teachers are not strict enough	☐	☐	☐	☐	☐
E.4	Modern methods are not used enough	☐	☐	☐	☐	☐
E.5	The teachers make me feel at home when I visit the school	☐	☐	☐	☐	☐
E.6	Not enough proper school work is done	☐	☐	☐	☐	☐
E.7	Parents have enough say in *what* their children are taught	☐	☐	☐	☐	☐
E.8	Parents have enough say in *how* their children are taught	☐	☐	☐	☐	☐

		Strongly agree	Agree	Don't know	Disagree	Strongly disagree
E.9	The school is traditional	☐	☐	☐	☐	☐
E.10	The teachers are capable of teaching my child without my help	☐	☐	☐	☐	☐
E.11	There is enough contact between the parents and the teachers	☐	☐	☐	☐	☐

F.1 How many times have you visited your child's school:

	1–3 times	4 or more	Not at all
in the last three months?	☐	☐	☐
in the last year?	☐	☐	☐
since your child started at this school?	☐	☐	☐

F.2 What is your occupation?
Mother ....
Father ....

F.3 How long have you lived in this county?

Less than 1 year	☐
1–3 years	☐
3 years or more	☐
born in this county	☐

F.4 At what age did you leave school?

	Age
Mother	☐
Father	☐

F.5 At what age would you like your child to leave school?

Age
☐

F.6 This form was completed by:

Mother	☐
Father	☐
Guardian	☐

F.7 If you were not born in this county, please state where you were born:
....

Thank you for helping with this inquiry. Kindly place this form in the envelope provided, seal it and send it back with your child to school. A box has been provided in which it can be placed. The results of this form are confidential and cannot be traced to individual parents. Please do not put your name or address on this form.

THANK YOU FOR YOUR HELP

Appendix III
Parent interview schedule

**Schools Council project 'Parents and Teachers: A Pilot Survey'
(based at University of Southampton)**

1 Full names of parents or guardians:
   Mother..
   Father..
   Address:..
   ....
   Length of time at present address: ....
   Previous address: ....
   ....

2 Children:

	Name	Age	Sex	School	Occupation	Age on leaving school
1	....	......	......	....	....	....
2	....	......	......	....	....	....
3	....	......	......	....	....	....
4	....	......	......	....	....	....
5	....	......	......	....	....	....
6	....	......	......	....	....	....
7	....	......	......	....	....	....

3 How important do you think your child's education will be in helping him to get on in the world?

4 What other things are important today in getting a good job for youngsters?

5 What do you think helps a child's education most, the school or the home background?

6 Does the school provide too many or too few occasions when you can visit the school to talk to the teachers?

7 Does the school provide you with enough information about what your child is being taught?

8 Does the school try to explain to parents some of the modern teaching methods used nowadays?

9 Could you suggest ways in which teachers could get to know parents better?

10 What do you think of parent–teacher associations?

11 Do you know anybody on the Board of Governors at your child's school?

12 Should the school be responsible for teaching children the difference between right and wrong or is that the responsibility of parents?

13 Would you like an occasional visit at home from one of your child's teachers?

14 Would you occasionally like to sit at the back of your child's class during an actual lesson to see how and what he is being taught?

15 Do you think schools should be used more for social and recreational purposes?

16   Do you think schools could be used to encourage a greater feeling of community in your neighbourhood?

17

	Occupation	Birthplace	Age completed full-time education
Father	....	....	....
Mother	....	....	....

18   Occupation of father's father:.......... ....

19   Occupation of mother's father:..

*

Date of interview...
Duration of interview ....
Persons present at interview...
Name of interviewer ....

Interviewer's comments:
....

Appendix IV
Questionnaire: survey of teachers' views on education

Schools Council project 'Parents and Teachers: A Pilot Survey' (based at University of Southampton)

School: .... Date: ....

Please tick here if you have attended any of the in-service sessions associated with the project: ☐

In the following questions please tick in each case the boxes which are RIGHT FOR YOU

A.1   Sex   Male   Female
           ☐   ☐

A.2   Status   Married   Single
           ☐   ☐

A.3   Present position at this school. Please state:
....

A.4   Age

20–24	25–29	30–34	35–39	40–44	45–49	50–54	55–59	60–65
☐	☐	☐	☐	☐	☐	☐	☐	☐

A.5   Number of years teaching:

	0–2	3–5	6–8	9–11	12+
in total	☐	☐	☐	☐	☐
at this school	☐	☐	☐	☐	☐

A.6   Please tick the appropriate boxes for those age groups of children which you have taught.

5–7	8–10	11–12	13–14	15–16	17–18
☐	☐	☐	☐	☐	☐

A.7 Please indicate, against the appropriate subjects, the age groups you have taught in school

	11–12	13–14	15–16	17–18
English	☐	☐	☐	☐
Music	☐	☐	☐	☐
Maths	☐	☐	☐	☐
Geography	☐	☐	☐	☐
History	☐	☐	☐	☐
Modern languages	☐	☐	☐	☐
P.E.	☐	☐	☐	☐
Art	☐	☐	☐	☐
R.I.	☐	☐	☐	☐
Wood, metal work	☐	☐	☐	☐
Business studies	☐	☐	☐	☐
Science	☐	☐	☐	☐
Domestic science	☐	☐	☐	☐
Other subjects	☐	☐	☐	☐

A.8 Have you children of your own?   Yes ☐   No ☐

A.9 If yes, then how many of each sex?   Boys ☐   Girls ☐

A.10 What are their ages? Please state:
Boys ....
Girls ....

A.11 For what age range of children did you train to teach?....................

A.12 For which school subject, if any, did you train to teach?
....

A.13 Are you a house tutor in this school at present?
Yes ☐   No ☐

A.14 Are you a form-master/mistress at present?   Yes ☐   No ☐

A.15 Please could you list other regular activities or responsibilities that you are involved in other than school-subject teaching? (e.g. producing school plays, in charge of a sports team, scouts, etc.)
....
....

Schools work in different ways without necessarily being better or worse than other schools. Here is a list of arrangements that some schools make. You will find that your school provides some and not others. Please read each item carefully and then tick the box which is *right for you.*

Does the school provide the following?	Too much provided	Enough provided	Don't know	Too little provided	Not provided
B.1 Open evenings	☐	☐	☐	☐	☐
B.2 Open days	☐	☐	☐	☐	☐
B.3 Talks for parents on education	☐	☐	☐	☐	☐
B.4 Opportunities for parents to talk to the headteacher	☐	☐	☐	☐	☐
B.5 Opportunities for parents to talk to the teacher	☐	☐	☐	☐	☐
B.6 A parents' or parent–teacher association (PTA)	☐	☐	☐	☐	☐
B.7 Opportunities for parents to help at school	☐	☐	☐	☐	☐
B.8 Information on how parents can help their child	☐	☐	☐	☐	☐
B.9 Opportunities for parents to help on school outings	☐	☐	☐	☐	☐
B.10 Other social functions for parents e.g. dances	☐	☐	☐	☐	☐
B.11 Hints on what books parents can get their child	☐	☐	☐	☐	☐
B.12 Evening classes for parents	☐	☐	☐	☐	☐
B.13 A newsletter/magazine	☐	☐	☐	☐	☐
B.14 Books for children to read at home	☐	☐	☐	☐	☐

Does the school provide the following?	Too much provided	Enough provided	Don't know	Too little provided	Not provided
B.15 Information for parents on what and how their child is taught	☐	☐	☐	☐	☐
B.16 Opportunities for parents to attend school assemblies	☐	☐	☐	☐	☐
B.17 Out-of-school activities during school holidays	☐	☐	☐	☐	☐
B.18 Information about the above activities	☐	☐	☐	☐	☐

PLEASE PUT YOUR TICKS IN THE BOXES WHICH ARE RIGHT FOR YOU

C.1 Generally speaking are you satisfied with home–school relations at your school?

Very satisfied ☐
Satisfied ☐
Not satisfied ☐

Every school has a board of managers or governors—

C.2 Do you know any of the school managers or governors?

All ☐
Some ☐
None ☐

C.3 Would you like to know who are the school managers or governors?

Yes ☐
No ☐

C.4 Should teachers be made managers or governors?

Yes ☐
No ☐

C.5 Should parents be made managers or governors?

Yes ☐
No ☐

C.6 Should pupils be elected to the board of governors?

Yes ☐
No ☐

C.7 Do you think the following should visit children's homes—

(*a*) The headteacher?

Yes ☐
No ☐
Don't know ☐

(*b*) The child's teacher?

Yes ☐
No ☐
Don't know ☐

(c) School counsellor (a teacher specially trained to help a child in difficulties)?

Yes ☐
No ☐
Don't know ☐

Please enter your answers here

C.8 What information would you like to have about the children that you teach, which you do not already have? ....

C.9 Is there anything taught in school which you think *should not* be taught? ....

C.10 Is there anything not taught in school which you think should be taught? ....

C.11 Describe briefly what you have heard about community schools, their advantages and disadvantages ....

If nothing, please tick ☐

C.12 Do you think your own school should develop into a community school?

Yes ☐
No ☐
Don't know ☐

We would like you to say how important you feel the following are for the school to try and do. In each case we should like you to tick the box you feel is right for you.

		Very important	Important	Don't know	Unimportant
D.1	Teach the child reading/writing/arithmetic	☐	☐	☐	☐
D.2	Help him/her to pass exams and to get a good job later	☐	☐	☐	☐
D.3	Help the child to be happy	☐	☐	☐	☐
D.4	Teach the child the difference between right and wrong	☐	☐	☐	☐
D.5	Teach him/her discipline	☐	☐	☐	☐

		Very important	Important	Don't know	Unimportant
D.6	Help the child to develop fully all his/her abilities	☐	☐	☐	☐
D.7	Develop respect for law and order	☐	☐	☐	☐
D.8	Develop his/her imagination	☐	☐	☐	☐
D.9	Teach him/her to enjoy leisure	☐	☐	☐	☐
D.10	Provide him/her with out-of-school activities, e.g. clubs	☐	☐	☐	☐
D.11	Prepare the child for being grown-up	☐	☐	☐	☐
D.12	Help parents to understand their children	☐	☐	☐	☐
D.13	Provide education for all the community including adults	☐	☐	☐	☐
D.14	Teach the child not to accept authority uncritically	☐	☐	☐	☐

Different parents have different opinions about schools. We should like you to read the following statements and then tick the ones which you feel apply to your school. [Question for teachers who were also parents.]

		Strongly agree	Agree	Don't know	Disagree	Strongly disagree
E.1	Most parents are happy with what the school is doing for the children	☐	☐	☐	☐	☐
E.2	The school is go-ahead	☐	☐	☐	☐	☐
E.3	Most teachers are not strict enough	☐	☐	☐	☐	☐
E.4	Modern methods are not used enough	☐	☐	☐	☐	☐

	Strongly agree	Agree	Don't know	Disagree	Strongly disagree
E.5 We make the parents feel at home when they visit the school	☐	☐	☐	☐	☐
E.6 Not enough basic school work is done	☐	☐	☐	☐	☐
E.7 Parents have enough say in *what* their children are taught	☐	☐	☐	☐	☐
E.8 Parents have enough say in *how* their children are taught	☐	☐	☐	☐	☐
E.9 The school is traditional	☐	☐	☐	☐	☐
E.10 We are capable of teaching the child without the parents' help	☐	☐	☐	☐	☐
E.11 There is enough contact between the parents and the teachers	☐	☐	☐	☐	☐

Much of our work on this project has been concerned with the development of links between the school and the community or the community school.

F.1 Do you feel this involves the teacher learning new skills?
Yes ☐   No ☐   Don't know ☐

F.2 Do you feel this involves a change of attitude on the part of teachers?
Yes ☐   No ☐   Don't know ☐

F.3 Do you think that courses could be provided to help in necessary changes?
Yes ☐   No ☐   Don't know ☐

F.4 What type of courses? Please specify. ....
....

F.5 To your knowledge, are these provided at the moment within your own area?
Yes ☐   No ☐   Don't know ☐

Thank you for helping with this inquiry. Kindly place this form in the stamped addressed envelope provided, seal it, and send it back to me. The results of this form are confidential and cannot be traced to individual teachers.

THANK YOU FOR YOUR HELP

Appendix V
In-service work questionnaire
(sent to teachers by group tutor)

Schools Council project 'Parents and Teachers: A Pilot Survey'
(based at University of Southampton)

School..

A   REACTIONS TO THE IN-SERVICE WORK

The first part of this questionnaire is aimed at helping me assess the work
which I did with you in the pilot project in-service work. If possible please
answer these questions regardless of the number of sessions which you
attended.

1   Number of sessions attended (circle one number).

3 or less	*1*
4–6	*2*
7–9	*3*
10–13	*4*
13 or more	*5*

2   If 9 or less, why was this?

little interest in topics	*1*
too many other commitments	*2*
other reason (please give it)	*3*

....

What is your personal view with regard to the following aspects of the course
as a whole? (Please circle one number for each separate question.)

Course organization

3   Prior knowledge assumed by the session was:

too much	*1*
about right	*2*
too little	*3*

4 Effort needed to follow arguments or exposition of ideas on average:
little effort   *1*
some effort, and unrewarding   *2*
some effort, but rewarding   *3*
too demanding   *4*

5 Organization of the *course as a whole:*
attended too few lectures to judge   *1*
insufficient linking structure or ideas   *2*
general structure or ideas were clear   *3*

6 The main emphasis of the course was:
too theoretical   *1*
an appropriate balance of theoretical and applied *2*
too applied   *3*

7 The course as a whole was:
satisfactory   *1*
well worth while   *2*
not worth while   *3*
unsatisfactory   *4*

8 If there are any more specific points which you would like to make about individual sessions these would be very welcome.

....

B EFFECT ON YOU

9 How much have you gained from the course as background for the understanding of significant educational issues?
Attended too few lectures to answer   *1*
A considerable amount (i.e. more than personal reading would
have achieved)   *2*
Some positive usefulness (i.e. enough to justify the time spent) *3*
Little or nothing (i.e. the work did not answer needs)   *4*

10 How much personal work have you done as a result of the course to increase your knowledge of the areas covered?
Selective study (e.g. reading emphasis on some areas of special
interest)   *1*
General study or reading only   *2*
Nothing   *3*

11 How satisfied did you feel with the balance struck between lecture/exposition (e.g. film, VTR, etc.) and discussion, on average?
Discussion given too much time   *1*
About right balance   *2*
Exposition/lecture, etc., given too much time   *3*

12 What do you think about the following aspects of the sessions? (Circle as appropriate.)

Should they have been more organized (e.g. with the tutor taking more of a 'leader' or specialist role)?   *yes/no*

Should the discussion have been more continuous from one session to the next?   *yes/no*

Should the groups have had specific tasks to accomplish?   *yes/no*

Did the sessions give you personally an opportunity for useful discussion?   *yes/no*

Did you feel that the sessions gave an opportunity for contrasting views to be heard and discussed?   *yes/no*

13 Did you find the second self-programming phase satisfactory?   *yes/no*

14 Please add below, if you wish, any comments or specific suggestions as to how the sessions could have been significantly improved or better adapted to *your* needs.

....

C POSSIBLE FOLLOW-UP ACTIVITIES

The following questions are an attempt to gauge what type of activities would find widest support and best meet the needs of teachers.

15 What type of work do you think would be most helpful to you within the field of the study of education in your job? (Please circle degree of usefulness as follows: *1*—very helpful; *2*—helpful; *3*—undecided; *4*—not helpful.)

(*a*) An interdisciplinary approach to various topics   *1 2 3 4*
(*b*) Psychological approach   *1 2 3 4*
(*c*) A sociological approach   *1 2 3 4*
(*d*) A philosophical approach   *1 2 3 4*
(*e*) An historical approach   *1 2 3 4*
(*f*) A study of a particular subject(s)   *1 2 3 4*

16 Which of the following areas/topics would you be most interested in studying further if given the opportunity? (Please circle the degree of interest as follows: *1*—very interested; *2*—fairly interested; *3*—undecided; *4*—not interested.)

(*a*) The school curriculum   *1 2 3 4*
(*b*) The pastoral role of the teacher   *1 2 3 4*
(*c*) Children's learning   *1 2 3 4*
(*d*) Group dynamics   *1 2 3 4*
(*e*) School organization (internal—e.g. streaming, setting, team teaching)   *1 2 3 4*

(f) School organization (external—e.g. types of schools, organization, etc.)   *1 2 3 4*

(g) The school's links with the community   *1 2 3 4*

(h) The school's links with other social services (e.g. probation, etc.)   *1 2 3 4*

(i) Any other aspect of school organization (please specify)

....

(j) Training for posts of responsibility   *1 2 3 4*

(k) Comprehensive education   *1 2 3 4*

(l) The upper secondary school   *1 2 3 4*

(m) The community school   *1 2 3 4*

(n) Welfare and back-up services   *1 2 3 4*

(o) The school, the home and the community   *1 2 3 4*

(p) Guidance and counselling   *1 2 3 4*

(q) Youth work   *1 2 3 4*

(r) Personality development in children   *1 2 3 4*

(s) Language development in children   *1 2 3 4*

(t) Development of thinking in children   *1 2 3 4*

(u) Programmed learning   *1 2 3 4*

(v) Compensatory education   *1 2 3 4*

(w) Objectives in teaching   *1 2 3 4*

(x) Social science and curriculum development in schools   *1 2 3 4*

(y) Instruction and discovery methods in teaching and learning   *1 2 3 4*

(z) Methods of investigation in education (e.g. testing, surveys, experimental design)   *1 2 3 4*

16 Any other topic(s)—please specify

....

....

17 Method of working. Which of the following methods of working do you prefer? (Please indicate degree of preference)

(a) Lecture method   *1 2 3 4*

(b) Small seminar (six to twelve persons)   *1 2 3 4*

(c) Larger seminar (thirteen to twenty persons)   *1 2 3 4*

(d) Discussion and consultation in schools   *1 2 3 4*

(e) A combination of the above   *1 2 3 4*

(f) Any other method of working (please specify)

....

D   LENGTH OF COURSE

18   Would you be willing to attend courses/meetings if they were offered on topics of interest to you at the following times? Please indicate degree of willingness/suitability: *1*—yes definitely; *2*—probably could; *3*—probably could not; *4*—no definitely.

(*a*) Evening meetings	*1*	*2*	*3*	*4*
(*b*) Saturday a.m.	*1*	*2*	*3*	*4*
(*c*) Saturday—all day	*1*	*2*	*3*	*4*
(*d*) Weekend residential	*1*	*2*	*3*	*4*
(*e*) Weekend non-residential	*1*	*2*	*3*	*4*
(*f*) Longer residential	*1*	*2*	*3*	*4*
(*g*) Day release	*1*	*2*	*3*	*4*
(*h*) Immediately at the end of afternoon school	*1*	*2*	*3*	*4*
(*i*) Across the lunch hour	*1*	*2*	*3*	*4*

19   To what extent would your attendance at courses/meetings be influenced by the possibility of acquiring further qualifications? Please indicate extent for (*a*) AND (*b*): *1*—to a considerable extent; *2*—to some extent; *3*—not at all.

(*a*) Shorter courses	*1*	*2*	*3*
(*b*) Longer courses	*1*	*2*	*3*

20   Which if any of the topics or groups of topics given in Section C do you think should be tailored to the acquisition of further qualifications?

....

E   RESEARCH AND FURTHER STUDY

21   Would you be interested in participating in some individual or group research work particularly of use to your own school? (Circle as appropriate.)   *yes/no*

22   Would you be willing to participate in a group/team research project, not necessarily linked with obtaining any qualification? (Circle as appropriate.)   *yes/no*

23   On which areas would you most like to undertake group or individual research? Please specify.

....

24   Would you be interested in information/advice with regard to how such research activities might also lead to further qualifications?   *yes/no*

25   Are you interested in the possibility of a part-time B.Ed. degree in the social aspects of education, if this were to become available to you? *yes/no*

26   Do you already have a university degree?   *yes/no*

27 If you do already have a university degree would you be interested in the possibility of a part-time master's degree in education with a social science bias, if this should become available?   *yes/no*
   If you would like to contact me separately on this question I should be pleased to advise you.

F   COMMENT

It is impossible to envisage through questions all of the different interests and aspirations of those who are taking part in the project. I should therefore be grateful for any further comments you may wish to make about this questionnaire, possible areas for future or follow-up courses or research projects which would be of use to teachers in their day-to-day work. May I thank you for the help which you have given.

....

PLEASE RETURN THIS QUESTIONNAIRE IN THE ENVELOPE
PROVIDED

Appendix VI
Suggestions for further reading

In his address to the National Confederation of Parent–Teacher Associations, 1973, Gerald Fowler suggested that:

Part of the obscurity of the controversy between those who advocate a conventional role for the school, the protagonists of 'free' schooling and the champions of 'de-schooling' . . . is that educational arguments become inextricably entangled with social arguments about the role of the school in the community.

Listed below, for those interested in following discussions concerning parental participation increasingly encountered in 'community development' debates, are a few selected publications suggested for further reading. Many of the works cited highlight both the desirability of parental involvement in the management of schools and the problem of parental choice and their child's school, which have caused heated arguments in recent years.

Many of the following works contain valuable bibliographies and readers are recommended to follow up references on aspects of parent–teacher relations which interest them. In addition, readers are referred to the three following bibliographies for a more detailed coverage of the topics.

Bibliographies

Goodacre, E. *Home and School Relationships: A List of References with Notes for Parents, Teachers and Teachers in Training.* Sheffield: Home and School Council, 1968.

Hooton, J. F. 'Selected Bibliography on Home and School Relationships.' *Aspects of Education*, 15, 1972, pp. 84–9.

Sharrock, A. N. *Home and School: a selected annotated bibliography.* Slough: National Foundation for Educational Research in England and Wales, 1971.

Books

Benn, C. and Simon, B. *Half Way There: Report on the British Comprehensive School Reform.* 2nd ed. Penguin Books, 1972.

Bond, G. *Parent–Teacher Partnership.* Evans, 1973.

Cave, R. G. *Partnership for Change: Parents and Schools.* Ward Lock Educational, 1970.

Central Advisory Council for Education (England). *Children and their Primary Schools* [The Plowden Report]. 2 Vols. HMSO, 1967.

Craft, M., Raynor, J. and Cohen, L. (eds.) *Linking Home and School.* Longmans, 1967.

Department of Education and Science. *Parent/Teacher Relations in Primary Schools* (Education Survey 5). HMSO. 1968.

Douglas, J. W. B. *The Home and the School.* MacGibbon & Kee, 1964.

Green, L. *Parents and Teachers: Partners or Rivals?* Allen & Unwin, 1968.

Kogan, M. and Van der Eyken, W. (eds.) *County Hall: The Role of the Chief Education Officer.* Penguin Books, 1973.

Mays, J. B. *The School in its Social Setting.* Longmans, 1967.

McGeeney, P. *Parents are Welcome.* Longmans, 1969.

Midwinter, E. *Patterns of Community Education.* Ward Lock Educational, 1973.

Morgan, C. *Community Involvement in Decision-making* (*Decision-making in British Education Systems*, Unit 13). Milton Keynes: Open University Press, 1974.

Sharrock, A. N. *Home/School Relations: their importance in education.* Macmillan, 1970.

Young, M. *Why our Susan?* Haringey Parents' Group/Advisory Centre for Education, 1969.

Periodical articles

Action issue: how to get things done. Where, 85, October 1973 (whole issue; seventeen articles.)

Armstrong, R. 'Towards the study of community action.' *Adult Education,* 45, May 1972, pp. 21–6. (Groups acting outside formal authority structures.)

Batten, T. R. 'The major issues and future direction of community development.' *Community Development Journal,* 9, April 1974, pp. 96–103.

Boothroyd, K. and Cohen, L. 'Willard Waller Revisited: Some Reflections on Parents' Expectations of Teachers.' *Journal of Curriculum Studies,* 4, November 1972, pp. 154–7.

Bosworth, D. P. 'Parents' attitudes to a programmed science course'. *Head Teachers' Review,* January 1974, pp. 21–2.

Bynner, J. 'Deprived parents.' *New Society,* 27, 21 February 1974, pp. 448–9. (Working-class parents' contacts with children's secondary schooling.)

Clarke, D. and others. 'Home and school relationships in action.' *Aspects of Education,* 15, 1972, pp. 35–65.

Cluderay, T. M. (ed.) 'Home and school relationship'. *Aspects of Education,* 15, 1972 (whole issue).

Cohen, L. and Boothroyd, K. 'Community expectations of the teacher's role: some mistaken perceptions of primary school teachers.' *Research in Education,* 7, May 1972, pp. 61–9.

'The cycle of deprivation.' Secretary of State's speech at the spring study seminar, on the Cycle of Deprivation, of the Association of Directors of Social

Services, Brighton, 27 March 1973. *Community Schools Gazette*, 67, May 1973, pp. 61–72. (Mainly on the possibility of breaking the cycle through better preparation for parenthood.)

Epstein, I., Tripodi, T., and Fellin, P. 'Community development programmes and their evaluation.' *Community Development Journal*, 8, January 1973, pp. 28–36. (Based on the authors' book *Social Programme Evaluation: guidelines for health, education and welfare administrators*—Itasca, Illinois: Peacock, 1971.)

Fryer, K. 'Parental involvement scheme. Infant/Junior.' *Remedial Education*, 8, 2, June 1973, pp. 35–6.

Grieve, J. 'The British Community Development Project: some interim comments.' *Community Development Journal*, 8, October 1973, pp. 118–25.

Griffiths, H. 'The aims and objectives of community development.' *Community Development Journal*, 9, April 1974, pp. 88–95. (Address given at a conference on Community Development and Education organized by Ayr County Council, November 1973.)

Hale, J. 'Parent-Teacher co-operation: an official view.' *Aspects of Education*, 15, 1972, pp. 70–83.

Harrison, J. 'Community work and adult education.' *Studies in Adult Education*, 6, April 1974, pp. 50–67. (The functions of community work and adult education for deprived groups.)

Hatch, S. and Moylan, S. 'The role of the community school.' *New Society*, 21, 21 September 1972, pp. 550–2.

'A hundred ways parents can help a school.' *Where*, 89, February 1974, pp. 43–5.

Jackson, K. and Ashcroft, B. 'Adult education, deprivation and community development—a critique.' Nuffield Teacher Enquiry, 1972, p(1), 19. Available from: The Secretary, University of York, York YO1 5DD. (Paper presented to a working group at the conference on 'Social deprivation and change in education' organized by the Nuffield Teacher Enquiry at the University of York, April 1972.)

King, R. 'Parents and schools.' *Secondary Education*, 2, 2, Spring 1972, pp. 29–30. (Report of a survey of secondary schools.)

Kirkpatrick, D. G. 'How close is American to British community development?—Some impressions.' *Community Development Journal*, 9, April 1974, pp. 108–16.

Lovett, T. 'Adult education and the community school.' *Community Development Journal*, 6, Autumn 1971, pp. 183–5.

Maddaford, C. A. 'International parent-teacher relations.' *Aspects of Education*, 15, 1972, pp. 66–9. (Work of international association in the field of parent-teacher relations.)

Marland, M. 'Notes they bring home.' *Where*, 86, 1973, pp. 322–4. (The quality of communication between schools and parents.)

McGeeney, P. 'A year's plan for a PTA: Getting off on the right foot.' *Where*, 61, September 1971, pp. 261–3.

—— 'A year's plan for a PTA: How we do things at this school.' *Where*, 63, November 1971, pp. 328–31.

—— 'A year's plan for a PTA: Inviting a guest speaker to the PTA.' *Where*, 64, December 1971, pp. 357–9.

—— 'A year's plan for a PTA: Raising cash.' *Where*, 65, January 1972, pp. 18–20.

—— 'A year's plan for a PTA: What sort of social occasions?' *Where*, 66, February 1972, pp. 58–60.

—— 'A year's plan for a PTA: I'm standing in the queue to see teacher.' *Where*, 67, March 1972, pp. 76–9.

McGeeney, P. 'Community Involvement and Educational Change.' *Forum*, 14, spring 1972, pp. 45–7.

Merson, M. W. and Campbell, R. J. 'Community education: instruction for inequality.' *Education for Teaching*, 93, spring 1974, pp. 43–9. (The problem of community education in inner cities, paying special attention to socially handicapped children.)

Moore, E. M. 'Human rights and home–school communications: a critical review.' *Educational Review*, 26, 1, November 1973, pp. 56–66.

Penn, R. 'Education—a social and political investment.' Available from: The Secretary, University of York, York YO1 5DD. (Report on the Community Development Project in Glyncorrwg, Glamorgan, including the community schooling approach: paper presented to the York conference—see entry for K. Jackson and B. Ashcroft, above.)

Pimlott, B. 'Who says working class mums don't want nursery education?' *Where*, 71, August 1972, pp. 213–15.

Punch, M. and Swirsky, R. 'Free but dead: why?' *Teacher*, 24, 6, 8 February 1974, pp. 3 & 15. (Reasons for the failure of the Scotland Road Free School, Liverpool.)

Reid, I. and Franklin, M. 'Comprehensive parents.' *New Society*, 24, 31 May 1973, pp. 488–90. (Characteristics of parents who choose comprehensive education rather than grammar school education for their children.)

Reid, I. and Franklin, M. 'Parental Choice between Grammar and Comprehensive in Mixed Systems.' *Comprehensive Education*, 23, spring 1973, pp. 5–8. (Characteristics of parents who choose comprehensive schools.)

Smith, M. 'Community development in New York City.' *Community Development Journal*, 8, October 1973, pp. 139–44.

Sofer, A. 'LEAs with parents as governors.' *Where*, 86, November 1973, pp. 326–9.

Stephens, E. and Wolpe, A. M. 'Two views on community schools.' *Times Educational Supplement*, 3037, 10 August 1973, p. 4. Comprises (1) 'U.S.: seeking to involve everybody', (2) 'Britain: close relationships with parents'.

Stephens, W. E. D. 'Some are more equal than others.' *Times Educational Supplement*, 3072, 12 April 1974, p. 21. (Argues that parental choice of school is harmful.)

Svendson, J. A. 'The responsibility of the counsellor/teacher in relation to the responsibility of the parent.' *Counsellor*, 17, March 1974, pp. 10–11.

Thorpe, E. 'Community schools—towards a definition.' *Education in the North*, 10, 1973, pp. 33–9.

Thurston, W. 'The community school concept: a personal view.' *Journal of*

Applied Educational Studies, **2**, 2, winter 1973, pp. 42–52. (Community schools in an Educational Priority Area.)

Town, S. W. 'Action research and social policy: some recent British experience.' *Sociological Review*, **21**, November 1973, pp. 573–98 (Studies the Educational Priority Area Project and the Community Development Project.)

Warrior, D. and Tuckwell, P. 'Home and school.' *New Society*, **22**, 19 October 1972, pp. 148–50.

Watt, J. 'Parent participation: why teachers are suspicious.' *Education in the North*, 10, 1973, pp. 5–8.

Will, D. S. 'Parents in the classroom—doubts dispelled.' *Education in the North*, 10, 1973, pp. 9–15.

Additional sources of information

Readers are reminded that many of the national organizations concerned with parent–teacher relations publish working papers, information sheets and periodicals, which can be obtained by writing to the addresses given below.

Advisory Centre for Education (ACE)
32, Trumpington Street,
Cambridge CB2 1QY   Tel. Cambridge 51456

Community Development Project,
Information Unit,
5, Tavistock Place,
London WC1H 9SS   Tel. 01–387 8622

Confederation for the Advancement of
State Education (CASE),
81, Rustlings Road,
Sheffield S11 7AB   Tel. Sheffield 662467

Home and School Council,
81, Rustlings Road,
Sheffield S11 7AB   Tel. Sheffield 662467

National Confederation of Parent–Teacher
Associations,
1, White Avenue,
Northfleet Gravesend, Kent.   Tel. Gravesend 60618

Pre-School Playgroups Association, Alford House,
Aveline Street,
London SE11 5DJ   Tel. 01–582 8871

Priority Area Children,
32, Trumpington Street,
Cambridge, CB2 IQY   Tel. Cambridge 51456

Appendix VII
Some useful films and where to obtain them

Test For Life
Sound. B & W. 50 mins.
Concord (BBC 1971), Concord Film Council Ltd, Nacton, Ipswich, Suffolk.

Learning by Doing (Discovery and Experience Series)
Sound. B & W. 30 mins.
Scottish Central Film Library, 16–17 Woodside Terrace, Charing Cross, Glasgow.

Counselling and Guidance (BBC Rosla Series)
Sound. B & W. 30 mins.
BBC TV Enterprises, Guild Sound and Vision, 85–129 Oundle Road, Peterborough, Northamptonshire.

Aims (Secondary Education) (BBC Rosla Series)
Sound. B & W. 30 mins.
BBC TV Enterprises.

School and Community
Sound. B & W. 30 mins.
BBC TV Enterprises.

All Together Now
16 mm B & W. 25 mins.
BBC TV Enterprises.

Willingly to School (Horizon Series)
Sound. B & W or Colour. 40 mins.
BBC TV Enterprises.

If At First You Don't Succeed—You Don't Succeed
Sound. B & W or Colour. 50 mins.
BBC TV Enterprises.